D0912414

A scene from "Holy Ghosts" at the Actor's Theatre of Louisville. Directed by Patrick Tovatt.

HOLY GHOSTS

BY ROMULUS LINNEY

★

DRAMATISTS
PLAY SERVICE
INC.

HOLY GHOSTS
Copyright © 1971, 1976, 1989, Romulus Linney

All Rights Reserved

SPECIAL NOTE

For Edgar and Amanda Loessin

HOLY GHOSTS was first produced in 1971 at East Carolina University, directed by Edgar Loessin, and in 1973 at the Garrick Theatre in New York, produced by Beth Grant. In 1976, after a production at the Cubiculo Theatre, it was published by Harcourt Brace Jovanovich, and subsequently staged by theatres large and small across the United States, including the Alley Theatre, The Actors Theatre of Louisville, the Birmingham Festival Theatre, the Detroit Repertory Theatre, and the San Diego Repertory, whose production was brought to New York for the 1987 Joyce Theatre Festival. With the following cast, directed by the author, it opened at the Alley Theatre on April 29, 1983.

NANCY SHEDMAN .... Cynthia Lammel
COLEMAN SHEDMAN .... Brandon Smith
ROGERS CANFIELD .... Timothy Arrington
OBEDIAH BUCKHORN, JR. .... Blue Deckert
VIRGIL TIDES .... David Radford
ORIN HART .... John Woodson
HOWARD RUDD .... James Belcher
LORENA COSBURG .... Laurel White
MRS. WALL .... Jo Marks
MURIEL BOGGS .... Dede Lowe
BILLY BOGGS .... William Johnson
OBEDIAH BUCKHORN, SR. .... Bob Burrus
CARL SPECTER .... Michael LaGue
BONNIE BRIDGE .... Robin Mosley
CANCER MAN .... Richard Hill

Directed by Romulus Linney
Setting by Keith Hein
Costumes by Ainslie G. Bruneau
Lighting by Sean Murphy
Sound by Tony Johnson
Production Stage Manager, Richard Earl Lester

CHARACTERS

NANCY SHEDMAN

COLEMAN SHEDMAN

ROGERS CANFIELD

OBEDIAH BUCKHORN, JUNIOR

VIRGIL TIDES

ORIN HART

HOWARD RUDD

LORENA COSBURG

MRS. WALL

MURIEL BOGGS

BILLY BOGGS

REVEREND OBEDIAH BUCKHORN, SENIOR

CARL SPECTER

BONNIE BRIDGE

CANCER MAN

PLACE

A one-room wooden building in the rural South.

TIME

The present: an evening in early summer.

HOLY GHOSTS

ACT I

The interior of a one room clapboard house located off a highway in the modern south. Some battered folding chairs are stacked against one wall. Other furniture, including an old piano, is covered by sheets and canvas.

On one bench, a young woman, Nancy Shedman, sits reading the Bible. A broom leans against the bench. She is reading aloud, slowly.

NANCY. So then — after the Lord has spoken to them — he was received up into heaven — and he sat on the right hand of God — And they went forth and preached everywhere — the Lord working with them — and confirming the word — with signs following. Amen. *(She stares at the Bible. She shakes her head, undecided about something.)* I want to stay here. With him. Don't I? Yes, Lord! Thank you, Lord! *(She closes the Bible and suddenly presses it fervently to her forehead. Then, briskly, she puts it down, picks up her broom, and goes back to work. She does not see a young man come quietly into the house. He watches her work. When she does see him, she lets out a cry, frightened.)*
COLEMAN. Hello, Nancy.
NANCY. Coleman!

COLEMAN. Oh, you Jezebel! Where's the man?

NANCY. He's not here, Coleman. But he will be! *(Backs away.)* He will be!

COLEMAN. *(Calling outside.)* Come on in, Canfield! We got her!

NANCY. Coleman, you can't come in here now.

COLEMAN. I'll do anything I want, Jezebel, after what you done to me! Canfield!

NANCY. *(Upset.)* Oh, *what* did I do to you, Coleman? *(Enter Canfield, and old man, cautiously.)*

COLEMAN. You know damn well. *(He moves toward her.)* I ought to knock your head off!

CANFIELD. No violence, son! That was the understanding! I have my heart condition. *(COLEMAN checks himself.)*

COLEMAN. All right. All right. *(Breathes deeply.)* I promised.

NANCY. Coleman, who's this man?

COLEMAN. My lawyer.

NANCY. Your what?

COLEMAN. My lawyer, god damn it! Who's going to defend me against your, oh, your deceit, and your treachery, and your god damned female bitchery!

CANFIELD. Son, that kind of language won't help.

COLEMAN. It'll help me, by God Almighty! Now lawyer, we've tracked her down. You heard her admit there's another man. Ain't that enough for a divorce?

NANCY. Divorce?

COLEMAN. What else, you flaming bitch?

CANFIELD. Well, not quite, son. It's just a little more complicated. *(To Nancy, with shaky charm.)* Madam, allow me to ask, are you Nancy Shedman, wife to Coleman Shedman?

NANCY. Yes, I am.

CANFIELD. Then let me say first, I regret the distress this meeting must cause you. Yet I feel certain we will all conduct ourselves here in a manner that can do credit to married ladies and gentlemen in an orderly and lawful civilization.

COLEMAN. Oh, fuck that, Canfield! Get down to business.

6

NANCY. Oh, you are so coarse! Coarse, and just downright repulsive!

COLEMAN. Coarse, am I? Repulsive, am I? Didn't you run out of our house with a man you never saw before? Tell the truth, Nancy! You been having carnal intercourse with the son of a bitch or not?

NANCY. I have not, Coleman, been doing what you say to no man! It is your ugly eyes looking out of your ugly face that sees ugly things. I did find a friend. I have entered into a tender human relationship.

COLEMAN. She's fucking him, Canfield. It's an open confession.

NANCY. It is not! It's the laying down of an unbearable burden. *(To Canfield.)* I can't help the mistake I made marrying this clod, who blackens every sweet thing he sees with his dirty, dusty mind.

COLEMAN. You hear how she talks to me? You hear how my wife talks to me?

CANFIELD. Yes, yes. Mrs. Shedman, would you consider discussing this other gentleman who has — ah — befriended you?

COLEMAN. That's it, Canfield! What's his name, Nancy?

NANCY. I'm not ashamed to tell you that, since he has asked me to marry him. His name is Obediah Buckhorn. He is a great preacher.

COLEMAN. I never heard of him.

NANCY. *(Angry)* Oh, Coleman, you are so dumb! You can't help it, and God have mercy on you, Coleman, but you are as dumb as a ditch! You are *the* fool of creation!

COLEMAN. Hear that? The fool of creation. Well, let me tell you this, Nancy. That preacher you ran off with, he ain't going to think I'm a fool, when I get my hands on him. I'm going to break his god damned neck. *(Enter Oby. He is a huge young man, with enormous muscles. He is handsome, cheerful, and self confident.)*

OBY. Good evening. God bless everyone here.

NANCY. Oby! *(She runs to him, throws herself into his arms. He puts one arm around her, and holds her protectively.)*

7

COLEMAN. See what I meant, Canfield? and me not even married to her a year. I'll be damned.

OBY. I hope not, Christian. I know you're Nancy's husband. You're angry now. I don't blame you for that.

COLEMAN. Wait a minute. How do you know I'm her husband? I never saw you before.

OBY. No, but I saw you Christian. That's why she's here, with us.

COLEMAN. Us?

NANCY. I been trying to tell you, Coleman. You won't listen, as always. There's more people *involved!* I am not going—

COLEMAN. Whoever's in on it! When I get through with you—

CANFIELD. No violence, son!

OBY. There won't be. I'm not a violent man, thank God. I don't like to fight, Christian.

COLEMAN. Maybe not, Christian, but you sure like to run off with other men's wives. And don't call me no Christian. I'm not one. Ain't Nancy told you what I think of that?

OBY. She has. I'm giving you the benefit of the doubt.

COLEMAN. Oh, you are? Well, all right, then, Christian! I beg everybody's pardon. I'm sorry to act up. No excuse for it. This man stole my wife, my furniture, my family heirlooms, and my Dodge pick-up truck. So praise God, Christian, what have I got to complain about?

OBY. *(Upset.)* Steal? Steal? *(To Nancy.)* Steal?

NANCY. We didn't, Oby.

COLEMAN. Steal, steal, steal, he's a parrot. He must be some stud, Nancy, to make up for it. Right?

NANCY. Coleman, you are the disgust of this world. Low down meaner than worms, you vile man. I will not talk to you further.

COLEMAN. That's why I got a lawyer. Canfield?

CANFIELD. Sensible young people. Let's sit down, and talk. Save everybody's time and money, and avoid going to court. Where I haven't been in so long anyway, I could make a lot of mistakes.

8

NANCY. Oby, .do we have time for this now? It'll just get more confused.

OBY. Whether we have time or not, I don't want anybody thinking I stole anything.

NANCY. All right, Coleman, your lawyer is trying to be civilized. I will do the same and serve coffee or tea. Which do you prefer, Mr. Canfield?

CANFIELD. Why, tea, Mrs. Shedman. I thank you.

NANCY. Not at all. Oby?

OBY. Tea, please.

NANCY. Coleman?

COLEMAN. God damn.

NANCY. That'll be three teas then. I got it right here.

COLEMAN. Aw, never mind no god damn tea party—

OBY. *(Firmly.)* Sit down.

CANFIELD. Do that, son. Just do that. *(Coleman sits, in disgust. Nancy fixes tea. Canfield takes out a pint bottle of whiskey.)* And I'll need a little of this to go with it, I'm afraid. I'm getting tired. Next thing, I'll have chest pains.

COLEMAN. Just a little now!

CANFIELD. Son, if I'm to maintain my legal efficiency, not to mention my mortal life, I got to have it. It keeps the big arteries loose and clear. Now, you want a lawyer, or not?

COLEMAN. All right, all right. *(Canfield takes a terrific snort of whiskey.)* Canfield! You can't knock back straight whiskey like that! You're too damn old. I don't want a lawyer dying on me!

OBY. You need to drink whiskey, my friend?

CANFIELD. I do. And God bless it. It loosens my heart.

OBY. Sorry to hear you say that. My Daddy would be, too. A man with heart trouble needs religion and healthy food, not whiskey. I eat soy beans and wheat protein. And look at me. *(Enter a young boy, Virgil Tides. He carries a wooden box. It is marked SHOTGUN SHELLS.)*

NANCY. Hello, Virgil.

VIRGIL. Hidy. I got them.

OBY. Set them down over there, Virgil. Out of the way.

NANCY. Want some tea?

VIRGIL. No, ma'am. *(He sets the box very carefully against one wall, and goes out.)*

COLEMAN. What the hell kind of strange kid was that?

NANCY. A dear friend, Coleman. Not some kid. Here's boneset tea for everybody. And sugar. And sugar spoons.

COLEMAN. My great grandmother's silver sugar spoons! Nancy, you stole every single thing of value right out of our house!

NANCY. Nobody stole nothing, Coleman!

CANFIELD. Now, young married people—

COLEMAN. That was just plain wrong!

CANFIELD. You see, the way we do this—

NANCY. It was a fair division of property!

COLEMAN. The hell it was!

CANFIELD. If you'll just listen in an orderly—

NANCY. And I earned every stick of it twenty times over!

COLEMAN. And I'm getting every stick of it back!

CANFIELD. There has to be some kind—

NANCY. Not one spoon! Not one shred of nothing, Coleman!

COLEMAN. All of it, Nancy! All of it!

CANFIELD. Hold it, youth! Just hold it! *(They do.)* Whew. There's a better way to do this. Believe me. *(To Coleman.)* Client, do you really want a divorce?

COLEMAN. I do.

CANFIELD. Mrs. Shedman, do you want a divorce?

NANCY. If he does. But I'm not giving him back—

COLEMAN. Oh, yes, you are!

CANFIELD. That comes later! Whew. First, we got to sort out the grounds for this action. Who did what to who and how, and so on.

COLEMAN. You sure you know what you're doing?

CANFIELD. Just trust me, son. Now, Mrs. Shedman—

NANCY. Call me Nancy.

CANFIELD. Now, Nancy—

COLEMAN. Canfield, whose side you on here, anyhow?

NANCY. Stop fighting with your own lawyer!

COLEMAN. I'm not! I'm just making damn sure you don't—

CANFIELD. Listen, youth! Just listen. We have to sort it out. Like this, now. *(He gets up. He takes a deep breath.)* My name is Rogers Canfield.

COLEMAN. I know that!

NANCY. Hush!

CANFIELD. Attorney at Law. In retirement, for my health. I am a widower.

COLEMAN. What the hell does that have to do—

NANCY. Just listen, Coleman!

CANFIELD. Procedure, son. Calm procedure. Thank you, Nancy.

NANCY. Don't mention it.

CANFIELD. I live with my daughter, who never married. In a little house. See, I've established these facts. Now, this morning, I was sitting on the porch, with nothing to do, looking at the road. Young Shedman came to see me. Clear so far?

NANCY. Yes, indeed.

COLEMAN. Yes, yes!

CANFIELD. He asked me if I knew a lawyer who could help him in his marital distress. I said I might. See how the facts can fall? Gently, and one at a time?

NANCY. I understand perfectly.

COLEMAN. So do I, So do I.

CANFIELD. Good. We're making progress. Mr. Shedman told me he didn't have much in the way of a fee. About that time, my daughter came out of the house, mad at me over something or other, said so, and went back in. I said, Mr. Shedman, get me off this porch today, and I'm yours. We made a deal. I'm out of legal retirement to serve him faithfully. That understood?

NANCY. Absolutely.

COLEMAN. Of course! Of course!

CANFIELD. Then you see how easy and gentle it can go. It's so simple. Just try it my way, young married people.

COLEMAN. OK. Fair enough. You first Nancy.

NANCY. No, you first, Coleman.

COLEMAN. Nancy—

NANCY. You started this action, Coleman!

CANFIELD. She has a point, son.

COLEMAN. Fine. I'll do it. I mean to be fair, Nancy, and right and honorable, and speak the truth.

CANFIELD. And that's a point for you.

NANCY. I'm listening.

CANFIELD. You see, we're doing all right. Son? *(Coleman gets up. He imitates Canfield.)*

COLEMAN. My name is Coleman Hannibal Shedman, Jr. I own and manage — *(Enter Virgil with another box. Coleman stares at him. He sets it carefully next to the first one, and exits.)*

NANCY. He'll be in and out, Coleman. Don't worry about him.

COLEMAN. I own and manage the Shedman Fish Farm, left me by my father when he died. I breed the finest lake stock in the South. It was a good life until one year ago, when like a fool, I wanted to get married. I met this woman, who said she loved me. But she didn't love me, not even from the very beginning! *(As Coleman talks, Nancy show signs of acute distress. It is difficult for her to listen without breaking in.)* Because, on our honeymoon, which I planned and planned to the last detail to please her, I took her all the way to Virginia! To camp there at beautiful Hungry Mother State Park! I bought us a brand new tent, planning for us to swim in the beautiful lake, and fish together, and I'd show her how to cook out, and then watch the sunset with my loving wife. But wrong again, Coleman. Because all she could say was, Hungry Mother is a stupid name for a State Park, and a miserable place for a Christian honeymoon, picking my plans all to pieces bit by bit, until there wasn't nothing left of what I tried to do for us but the inside of that tent, as black as blackest night. And it was more of the same almost for one whole year, until one week ago.

NANCY. All right, all right now!

COLEMAN. I come home that night. I was emotional, upset, full of misguided love. I took Nancy tenderly in my arms, and tried to tell her how much I cared.

NANCY. Oh, my God!

COLEMAN. But I was tired! Working and slaving to support my wife at the fish farm. I fell asleep. And when I woke up the next morning, wife, furniture, family heirlooms, and my Dodge pick-up truck, gone. Gone! In their place, a little note. "Dear Coleman. Last night I met a real man. Yours truly, Nancy." Well, all right. But god damn it, I want all my family furniture, and my family heirlooms, and my pick-up truck, and a divorce! My wife and Mr. Soy Bean can have each other, I'll live with Daddy's fish! They treat me better than she ever did! *(He sits down. NANCY jumps up.)*

NANCY. Oh boy, Coleman! Oh boy, Coleman!

CANFIELD. Gently, now! Sensible married people. Gently.

NANCY. My name may be Nancy Shedman, but I'm not yours no more, Coleman, you frog. Not in no way, shape or form!

COLEMAN. Is that a god damn promise?

NANCY. It certainly is, and has been, since that same night you have described out of the folly of your twisted mouth.

COLEMAN. Hear that? Twisted mouth.

NANCY. Because a lot more happened that night than you'll admit, Coleman, you horse-faced rat and rodent, you.

COLEMAN. Horse-faced rat and rodent. Hear that?

CANFIELD. Now, gently, sensible young—

NANCY. You come home, all right. Looking like you always do, puffed up mad at the world, and me in it. You weren't full of misguided love, you were full of beer and whiskey! You wouldn't say a word. Just mope around, and mope around, and then boom! All of a sudden grabbing me. Hauling me down on the sofa, like a sack of potatoes. Starting in on me until I myself, in spite of myself, was swept with carnal desire. When I finally managed to get my clothes decently off, you pawing and clutching, and finally got my desires decently ready for you, I said so. Because I wanted you, Coleman, because I want a *baby*, Coleman, a *baby*, and said so! Then, you climbing on top of me on that old sofa and just hanging there. Then passing out! Out, just plain out, *boom!* Like that. Me rolling humiliated out from under you, and letting you flop, *boom!* your big stuffed head going down like a rock, hitting the coffee table, *boom!*

like that, splitting your lip, and me wishing you'd split your brains and broke your neck! Oh, Coleman, Oh, Coleman! You don't know what it's like, to be a mortified wife. I felt so bad. Dear Jesus, I prayed, give me a sign. And about that time, you snorted, and rolled over on your back on the floor, *flop!* like that, with your pants down and that thing of yours sleeping just like you, *flop!* *(Listening to this, Coleman has been going crazy. Now he sees a large, rough looking man, Orin Hart, enter. Hart is looking anxiously for someone he missed on the way, hoped would be there and isn't. Disappointed, he sits alone on a bench.)*

COLEMAN. Who's that man?

NANCY. Oh, hush! There I was, naked in my own living room, with my husband passed out on the floor. Again. Because that's what always happens, since that campfire honeymoon of his. Instead of decent married relations, it's him get drunk, me want a baby, *boom!* and *flop!* It was such a mess. I wanted to die. I hadn't even noticed he'd left the front door open. Somebody was there. I turned around, crying. It was Oby.

COLEMAN. Doing what, preacher? Whacking off?

OBY. Now, hold on—

NANCY. Asking me politely, Coleman, if I had a kitchen match. So he could light his campfire down by the river. So understanding and polite about the fact I didn't have my clothes on, so gentle and kindly faced.

COLEMAN. He ain't kindly faced. He ain't nothing faced. He's so god damned dumb nothing registers there at all.

NANCY. I register there! Your wife registers there, and likes it a lot. *(To Canfield.)* Oby waited while I put on my clothes. I got his matches. And I went with him to his campfire. And it was so different. A different campfire from any of yours, Coleman. I told Oby everything. He understood. And he told me things, about life, and Jesus our Lord, and the Bible, things I sure never heard before anywhere. And he took me in his manly arms, and said a prayer in my ear, and kissed me. And then, oh! what a difference, between *(Pointing at Oby.)* day and *(Pointing to Coleman.)* night! *(Another tough looking man, Howard Rudd, enters. He is not as big as Hart, but he is just as rough.)*

OBY. *(To Rudd.)* Sit down anywheres. We'll be through in no time.

RUDD. *(Distracted.)* Is Orin here? *(Hart sees Rudd and Rudd sees Hart. They rush to each other, and embrace.)*

HART. I thought you wasn't coming!

RUDD. I waited half an hour at the pool room!

HART. Pool room? I thought you said meet here!

RUDD. No, no, we were supposed to meet there and come here later!

HART. Who said that?

RUDD. You did.

HART. No, I didn't! What I said was— *(Rudd grabs Hart.)*

RUDD. Well, never mind! I'm sorry if I messed up.

HART. No, I did. Just so you're here.

RUDD. I am.

HART. It's all right, then. Everything's all right. *(They kiss. A pale, drab, very worried little middle aged lady, Lorena Cosburg, enters timidly.)*

LORENA. Oh, I'm sorry! I thought there was a church service here. I don't mean to intrude. *(She turns to go.)*

OBY. You're not intruding, ma'am. Come right in and sit down. It'll begin shortly.

COLEMAN. Wait a minute. Two men are hugging and kissing each other back there.

NANCY. Just let me finish. I came back to the house with Oby, happy for the first time in my woman's life. And you still passed out on the floor. I said, "Listen, Oby, I have earned freedom, a fair division of furniture, and transportation, too." So we loaded everything I wanted over your head, out the door, and put it in your filthy old truck, and drove off. To here. Where I stand now, defying you, Coleman, you dog. By the way, I sold your truck. *(A large woman named Mrs. Wall walks impressively in. She waves to Nancy.)* Hidy.

MRS. WALL. Hello, Nancy. You sweet thing. Praise the Lord.

15

COLEMAN. Now who for god's sake is that?

NANCY. Mrs. Wall.

COLEMAN. Mrs. who?

MRS. WALL. Wall! Wall!

COLEMAN. Two men hugging each other, and a woman named Wall. *(Mrs. Wall removes a sheet, revealing a battered upright piano. She settles herself there.)*

NANCY. She's a sweet Christian companion and friend. Never you mind about her name. So, Mr. Canfield, that is my story. Do you understand everything now?

CANFIELD. I fear I am beginning to, yes.

COLEMAN. *(To Oby.)* All right, Soy Bean. Your turn.

OBY. Me?

COLEMAN. We get to hear your story of what happened on that fateful night. *(Looks at the people.)* All fifty of us, or however the hell many people we got in here now. O my god! *(A young man, Billy Boggs, with a guitar, enters. With him is his young wife, Muriel, with a baby in her arms.)*

MURIEL. Hey, Nancy.

NANCY. Muriel! You brought the baby!

MURIEL. I sure did!

NANCY. *(To the baby.)* Why, he's just the sweetest thing! Hey, there! Hey, honey! Whoo-hoo! Buba-buba-boo! Oh, Lord, Muriel, he's nice.

MURIEL. Yes, he is. *(Billy hits a note on Mrs. Wall's piano, and tunes one string of his guitar. Mrs. Wall joins Nancy and Muriel, looking at the baby.)*

BILLY. *(To Coleman.)* Hi. *(He moves away, tuning his guitar.)*

COLEMAN. Elvis Presley. My god. Hey, Soy Bean! *(Smiling, at ease, Oby goes to Canfield.)*

OBY. You want to hear my story, here it is, cross my heart and hope to die. *(To Canfield.)* It started when I got laid off my full time job at the Skyrocket Bowling Alley. Couldn't get along with the manager. I went up in the mountains to think about it, and fish, and pray. I was camping by Caesar's Creek, just above Stone Mountain River. I went to cook my trout. I'd run out of matches. I'd seen this

16

little house up by the road. I went and looked, and there was a light on inside. The front door was open. I looked in. There, without any clothes on, was a fine young lady. *(Oby smiles, and spreads his hands. He appreciates the absurdity of the occasion.)* I said, "Ah, hello. You got a match?" And she said maybe she did. When I told her what I wanted it for, she said if I could wait until she put some clothes on, she'd not only give me a box of matches, she'd come down and cook my trout for me. And she did. *(To Coleman.)* And told me about you.

COLEMAN. What about me, Soy Bean?

OBY. Enough. You want to know why she likes my campfire better than yours? Because I know that God Himself is always the other person around any fire. Any fire. She understands that now, too. *(To Canfield again.)* She asked me what to do about her husband. I said, "Go ask my Daddy. He preaches about men and women all the time. He knows more than I do." She said that sounded like a good idea. She had a pick-up truck and some furniture she wanted to take with her. Fine. Well, Daddy liked her right off. So much, he offered her the back room over the kitchen in our house, for as long as she wants it. Folks often stay with us from time to time. Ask around, lawyer. You will find we are respected Christian people. Nothing wrong has been done. And, since then, I've been looking for a steady job. Today, I got one. I can't wait to tell my Daddy about it. *(Smiling with anticipation, he sits down.)*

COLEMAN. How about it, Canfield? Read between the lines. If that ain't enough for a divorce, what is? *(Sounds of guitar, piano chords. The people chat with each other, moving about, friendly, but not gushing. They are at ease but it is evident they are all here for a serious purpose.)*

CANFIELD. My goodness. Just look at these people.

COLEMAN. Listen, Oby. Are you trying to tell me that instead of having carnal relations with my wife, when she was wide open, if you can pardon the expression, you took her instead to see your Daddy?

OBY. That's right.

COLEMAN. Then what the hell are you doing, pimping for

your Daddy?

NANCY. Coleman—

COLEMAN. And what kind of grown-up man lives with his Daddy, anyhow? Great God Almighty, if my old man and me lived in the same house one day after I hit sixteen, they'd a buried the both of us.

NANCY. Coleman—

COLEMAN. *(To Oby.)* But not you. You live with Daddy.

NANCY. Coleman—

COLEMAN. *(To Nancy.)* And so do you, now! When you marry him, you still gonna live with Daddy?

NANCY. Coleman—

COLEMAN. Well, what is it, Nancy? Speak up!

NANCY. Coleman, you are the one who's insisted all this time I am going to marry Oby.

COLEMAN. Huh?

NANCY. I'm not.

COLEMAN. Huh?

NANCY. Oby is my dear friend and brother in the Lord, but he is not my happiness. He brought me to it, but he is not the thing itself.

COLEMAN. Wait a minute. You said you was going to marry Obediah Buckhorn.

NANCY. Yes. Obediah Buckhorn, Senior.

OBY. *(Smiling.)* Daddy.

COLEMAN. *Daddy??* You marrying his *Daddy?*

NANCY. Yes!! Finally, Coleman, whew!! That's it!

COLEMAN. Well, god-a-odd-damn! Daddy, eh? Canfield, my fine young wife left me for Daddy. Well, where is he? Let's all have a look at Daddy. Daddy! Yoo-hoo! Daddy? Where in hell is he, anyhow?

BUCKHORN. Right here. God bless you, son. *(He has just entered.)*

COLEMAN. Him?

NANCY. Him. *(She goes to the Reverend Buckhorn, and stands beside him.)* At last you got here. It's my husband. *(To Coleman.)* The

18

Reverend Buckhorn will take care of everything now, Coleman.

COLEMAN. You going to marry this old man? *(To Buckhorn.)* Daddy, I can put your ass in jail. For it seems you and your idjit son here have stole my wife.

BUCKHORN. I can see you mean to test me, son.

COLEMAN. And fucking how. This is my lawyer, and we got you dead to rights.

BUCKHORN. I understand how you must feel. Life is hard.

COLEMAN. You hear that son of a bitch say to me? I'm gonna—

CANFIELD. Son! No violence!

BUCKHORN. But your wife came to us of her own free will. And suffering, because of you. *(To Nancy.)* And her own ignorance.

NANCY. *(Head bowed.)* Yes, Lord.

BUCKHORN. All your questions, Mr. Sedman, will be answered. But we have a service to the Lord God to celebrate here tonight, and every thing else must wait upon that. You will know everything you want to know. *After* the worship. Excuse me. *(He brushes past Coleman and kisses Oby fondly, and then Nancy affectionately but with a gleam in his eye, too. Then he moves away, welcoming the others, who are all waiting to greet him.)*

COLEMAN. Lawyer! What are we going to do about it?

CANFIELD. Well— *(Enter Carl Specter. He is a very strange, raw boned country man. He sees Coleman, someone new, and goes to him, talking.)*

CARL. She come into my life from nowhere, don't you see? I found her in the city dump, dying in a shoebox, with all her dead little brothers and sisters around her. But she was still alive. I took her home. I fed her cornbread and milk. And she lived. *(He nods at Coleman, having said something tremendous.)* She lived! *(He turns to others, who nod protectively. Coleman shakes his head.)*

COLEMAN. What was *he* talking about?

NANCY. About his phantom setter. That's Carl Specter, talking about his phantom setter.

COLEMAN. His what?

NANCY. A bird dog, Coleman, who died. He's a man haunted by his dog. Can't you understand that?

COLEMAN. Well, of course, Nancy. Sure. Hell, yes.

NANCY. Coleman, since I left you, and came to live with Reverend Buckhorn, I see how limited you really are. You can't tolerate nothing in the slightest human way unusual. You have got a lot to learn. *(Enter Bonnie Bridge. In her early forties, she is very attractive. On the surface she is practical, efficient and cheerful.)*

BONNIE. How are you, Nancy?

NANCY. Fine, Bonnie. How're you?

BONNIE. Doing all right, praise the Lord. *(To Coleman and Canfield.)* Hello. Welcome to our church. If you could give me your names, I'll see that you're properly introduced to everyone before we begin. *(To Coleman.)* What's your name, young man? Don't be shy.

COLEMAN. God damn it, Nancy.

BONNIE. *(Understanding.)* Oh, Nancy, it's your husband.

NANCY. I'm afraid so.

BONNIE. I should have known. *(To Coleman.)* You're not here for church, then.

COLEMAN. I'm here for a divorce. This is my lawyer. *(Canfield quickly extends his hand.)*

CANFIELD. My name is Rogers Canfield. Very pleased to meet you.

BONNIE. Mine is Bonnie Bridge. God bless you, sir.

CANFIELD. Thank you. God bless you, too. *(She smiles at Canfield, and moves away to other people. Canfield stares after her.)*

COLEMAN. Canfield!

NANCY. Mr. Canfield, can we finish, please?

CANFIELD. Well. *(To Coleman.)* I doubt if you could prove adultery, now. *(To Nancy.)* But if the wife admits desertion, the husband does have grounds for divorce, and is entitled to all his property.

NANCY. Wait a minute! Who admits desertion? I left this man by the right of suffering. I had to find some decent joy and beauty in my life. Every woman has a right to that. I don't owe this fool a thing more than what he owes me: one wasted year of our lives! I'm not giving him back nothing!

COLEMAN. That's what you think, Nancy.

NANCY. That's what I know, Coleman. Now you just get out of here. We've given you all the time we can.

BUCKHORN. I think we're ready, now. Have you finished your talk?

OBY. Yes, sir.

NANCY. Yes, sir.

BUCKHORN. Good. Is Cancer Man here yet?

OBY. No, sir.

BUCKHORN. We'll wait then, a few minutes. I wouldn't want to start without him. *(He moves away again.)*

COLEMAN. Cancer Man?

NANCY. Yes, Coleman.

COLEMAN. *Cancer Man?*

NANCY. Yes, yes! Can't you understand English? A man who has cancer. He comes here because it helps him. He don't have no place else to go.

COLEMAN. If he has cancer, why doesn't he go to a hospital?

NANCY. Coleman, you don't know what you're talking about.

COLEMAN. Oh? *(Hurt.)* Didn't my Mama die of it when I was a boy? And didn't I take my Daddy to the hospital with it not two years ago?

NANCY. Yes. I forgot. I'm sorry.

COLEMAN. Didn't I see them waste away to nothing? Didn't I watch Daddy die, not even know who I was? His own son? *(Enter Cancer Man. He is a sick man in late middle age. The sight of him reminds Coleman of his father, and it frightens him.)*

CANCER MAN. Hidy.

BUCKHORN. Hello, Cancer Man. We been waiting for you.

CANCER MAN. Have you? Waiting for me? God bless you for that. What would we do, if we couldn't come to church? *(He sees Coleman. He holds out a hand to him.)* Hello, son.

COLEMAN. *(Hushed.)* You got cancer?

21

CANCER MAN. *(Simply.)* Yes. *(Coleman turns away from him, abruptly.)*

BUCKHORN. Now, friends. Let's start the worship. Begin. *(The people move now, quickly. Mrs. Wall plays "Amazing Grace." and they sing it heartily, as they change the room about. A table is brought to the middle of the room. It becomes an altar. On it is placed a rough wooden cross. A mason jar of clouded liquid is placed very carefully by the cross. The wooden boxes are put before the altar. A large sign goes up:*

```
AMALGAMATION

HOLINESS

CHURCH OF GOD

WITH SIGNS

FOLLOWING
```

While this is happening, Coleman follows Nancy, who helps with the setting up of the church.)

COLEMAN. Wait a minute, Nancy? What about the divorce? What about my property? What about this old man you're going to marry? You lost your mind? Bunch of lunatics in here: Two truck-drivers hugging and kissing each other? Another man talking to a dead dog? Another man dancing around saying he's got cancer? What kind of religion is this, anyhow? Nancy, what's happened to you? Nancy? *(Nobody pays him any attention. They are all cheerfully singing "Amazing Grace," and getting ready for church.)*

ALL. *(Singing.)*

Amazing Grace, how sweet the sound
That saved a wretch like me,
I once was lost but now am found,
Was blind, but now I see.

Twas grace that taught my heart to fear,

And grace my fears relieved,
How precious did that grace appear,
The hour I first believed.

Through many dangers, toils, and snares,
I have already come,
Tis grace hath brought me safe thus far,
And grace will lead me home.

When we've been there ten thousand years,
Bright shining as the sun,
We've no less days to sing God's praise,
Than when we first begun.

Amazing Grace, how sweet the sound
That saved a wretch like me,
I once was lost, but now am found,
Was blind, but now I see.

(They settle. Crude lights have been turned on. There is no formal arrangement of the congregation. They sit scattered informally about the room. In front of the altar however, a space is left open.)

BUCKHORN. Now, folks. Before ary other thang, it is I myself must declare myself here to you! I would hold nothing back!

CONGREGATION. Amen, brother.

COLEMAN. A-fucking men, and how, brother.

BUCKHORN. *(Pause — deep breath.)* You all do know the sunshine that has come into my life. This young and tender maiden—

COLEMAN. Maiden? Hoo!

BUCKHORN. *(Pause — deep breath.)* Who came to me lost and forlorn, ravaged by the brutality and the squalor of godless wedlock, her lovely womanly—

COLEMAN. Wedlock is right, brother. Wait til it snaps on you.

BUCKHORN. *(Pause — deep breath.)* Her lovely womanly spirit crushed, her gentle nature defiled, her trusting heart broken—

COLEMAN. And pissed off, in the bargain.

BUCKHORN. Came here to me, and to our church, and asked us for help, for guidance, for love and faith. and you gave, and I gave—

COLEMAN. And she gave—

BUCKHORN. And she was healed! Made whole! Sound! Radiant with the spirit of the Lord! Is this ary kind of lie? Speak, little Nancy! Speak the truth!

NANCY. *(Simply, sincerely.)* I was lost, but now am found. Was blind, but now I see. You have given me back my life.

BUCKHORN. Thank you for that. *(To Congregation.)* And it is no secret here, that my feelings for this girl have become, in the way of mortal men, matrimonial. Her youth and sunshine for me, my strength and experience for her.

COLEMAN. God damn.

BUCKHORN. Here is her husband, come cursing amongst us. You see the man. With rage, tight as a tick. Now, Mr. Shedman. You may not believe this, but everybody here comprehends your extreme married misery. Including me. Nobody belittles it. Including me. As soon as I can, when service is over, I will have everything out with you. But first things come first. Til church is over, you are our friend and guest. We beg you stay, and be welcome! *(To Canfield.)* And you are welcome, too. *(To the congregation.)* Isn't that right?

ALL. Why, yes! It certainly is! Yes, indeed. Welcome, friends.

CANFIELD. That's very decent of you. Much obliged. *(To Coleman.)* Have a seat, son.

COLEMAN. What, listen to this?

CANFIELD. You have to. Don't you want your settlement? Your property back?

COLEMAN. Oh, yeah. Damn right I do. OK. *(Music. Chords on the paino, from the electric guitar. Perhaps a harmonica, a tambourine, whatever they would play. Led by Billy and Mrs. Wall, they supply their own music very well.)*

CANFIELD. Just be patient.

COLEMAN. Oh, sure. *(He slips the whiskey bottle from Canfield's pocket, and takes a quick drink.)* Want some?

CANFIELD. No, thanks.

COLEMAN. Huh?

CANFIELD. Put that away, son. We're in church.

COLEMAN. What about your heart condition?

CANFIELD. I'll chance it. Now, hush up. *(They are seated to one side. Buckhorn is now walking about, listening to the music.)*

BUCKHORN. *(Easily.)* Well, what is real religion? One thing I know, it don't have no beginning, and it don't have no end. It is happening all the time, and tonight I hope it will happen to us. *(He listens, and smiles.)* That sounds good, Billy. Mrs. Wall. I hope we have good music tonight, to the glory of God. I think we will. Mr. Hart. Mrs. Rudd. Carl. God bless all of you, my friends. *(He turns to Bonnie.)* Miss Bridge?

BONNIE. Friends, the Kiley Haines family were burned out of their house last night. They weren't hurt, but their clothes went up with everything else. *(Holding a piece of paper.)* I have the children's sizes here. If you'll look at them later on, and bring in what you can, I'll see they get it. *(People respond: they will.)* We have three new faces with us tonight. First of all — where are you? *(Looks.)* Oh, there you are. Come on out. A new friend, Mrs. Lorena Cosburg. *(Lorena steps shyly forward.)*

ALL. Welcome. Hidy!

LORENA. Hello. *(She moves back quickly.)*

BONNIE. This gentleman is Mr. Coleman Shedman. He is Nancy's husband.

ALL. Welcome. Hidy!

COLEMAN. *(A mock bow.)* Oh, how do you do?

BONNIE. And last, but certainly not least, a distinguished lawyer, Mr. Rogers Canfield.

ALL. Welcome. Hidy!

CANFIELD. *(Very pleased.)* I'm happy to be here. *(He smiles at Bonnie, who smiles back.)*

BONNIE. And I have the latest about Gilbert Letty. He's out of the hospital. He's home now, with Martha. He's still in pain, but not in agony like he was. He'd welcome visits from comforting friends. And Reverend Buckhorn, may I say this?

BUCKHORN. Of course.

BONNIE. You all know what happened to me here. How sick I was over it for so long. Let me tell you, I appreciated your visits and your prayers. I know now how the sick and the needy feel. And — oh, Lord — now I want to pray!

BUCKHORN. Then do. *(She prays aloud, fervently.)*

BONNIE. Oh, Lord Jesus, I was so sick! I wanted to die so many times, and you heard my prayers and brought my friends to help me, and so, Lord, I pray now that you will send health and mercy to Gilbert Letty and his wife and children! And to all the sick and needy people in this world! *(Others join her, each with his own prayer. In a moment, the whole congregation is praying aloud and with real passion, for the afflicted. Many are on their knees. With a look at Coleman, Nancy falls to her knees and prays for him.)*

NANCY. Oh, Lord! Let me pray to you right now, for my husband, Coleman! Forgive my evil thoughts against him! You know I can't stand him anymore, and he is a terrible mess, but maybe he can't help that, Lord, and I pray that you will come into his life and do him some good and show him the way! Amen, Lord Jesus! *(With another look, she gets up and walks away, to Oby. Coleman, staring at them all, throws up his hands. The prayers, a few at a time, end. When they are all quite finished, Buckhorn speaks again.)*

BUCKHORN. Now folks, I see Muriel and Billy Boggs there with some good news. Billy? *(Billy, the young man who plays the electric guitar, gets up, a little reluctantly.)*

BILLY. Well, we had the baby, as you know. She's got it with her. Muriel? *(His pretty young wife stands up, happy. She holds her baby, who has been nursing at her breast.)*

MURIEL. He's only three weeks old. I wanted to bring him here quick as I could. Edward William Boggs. Billy has nicknamed him Wrinkle. That's because the first day we had him home, Billy didn't see him where I had him under a bedsheet, and almost sat on him. He said he looked like just another wrinkle in the sheets. And that's what he was. You all know we never meant to have him this fast. But we're happy about it, anyhow. Ain't we, Billy?

BILLY. Yeah.

MURIEL. He already has a godmother. Elrita Moss, who won't come here, I'm sorry to say. But he needs a godfather, for the years ahead. *(She goes to Cancer Man.)* Will you do that for us? I believe you will get well, and live for many years. He might need somebody like you, who is good and wise.

CANCER MAN. You people here. You are the best things in the world to me. *(Moved, he holds up his hands to take the baby, but very shyly.)*

MURIEL. Here. Don't be afraid to hold him. You won't scare him. He'll know you love him. *(Cancer Man takes the baby in his arms.)*

CANCER MAN. I thank you, Lord Jesus. Little boy, I will stand by you, as long as I live. Bless you, child. All the days of your sweet young life.

BUCKHORN. What a fine thing. You know, Jesus was a baby like this, once. How we love that. Baby Jesus. Mrs. Wall, play us some Baby Jesus music. Billy, you proud Daddy. Sing, friends. *(Mrs. Wall plays "Fairest Lord Jesus." The people gather around Muriel and sing it to the baby, and to her. Coleman stares at them, shaking his head.)*

COLEMAN. Canfield, there is something wrong about these people. I just feel it.

ALL. *(Singing gently.)*
Fairest Lord Jesus, ruler of all nature,
O Thou of God and man the son,
Thee will I cherish, Thee will I honor,
Thou my soul's glory, joy, and crown.

COLEMAN. I mean, they're not all right in the head. *(Looks around.)* And this place. I mean, what kind of church is this?

ALL. *(Singing.)*
Fair is the sunshine. Fairer still the moonlight.
And all the twinkling, starry host.
Jesus is fairer, Jesus is purer,
Than all the angels heaven can boast.

COLEMAN. What are they doing up there, pretending that

damn baby is Jesus? I tell you, something is dead wrong about this whole thing. *(The song ends. Cancer Man approaches Coleman.)*

CANCER MAN. Son?

COLEMAN. Oh, my god.

CANCER MAN. Don't you want to see the baby?

COLEMAN. No, I don't.

CANCER MAN. Why not? Pretty child. Don't you like children?

COLEMAN. What business is that of yours? What do you care if I like children or not?

CANCER MAN. I like you. I want to be your friend.

COLEMAN. Well, thank you, but I'm not interested. Look, it's too bad you're sick.

CANCER MAN. Don't worry about it. I don't.

COLEMAN. Of course not. Will you just please leave me alone?

CANCER MAN. All right. I am sorry I have troubled you. *(Cancer Man goes back to the others. Coleman sees Canfield looking at him with disapproval.)*

COLEMAN. What are you looking at?

CANFIELD. Nothing, son.

COLEMAN. By God, I don't see why everybody had to call me son around here. *(He steps to the center of the room.)* And I've had about enough of this! Nancy, there ain't nothing more happening in here until we get through! You can sing hymns til hell freezes over. I don't care! You can marry Oby, Daddy, or the milkman. I don't care! *(He looks about, sees the boxes in front of the table, marches over and sits on them.)* But I ain't waiting no longer. I'm here to get what's coming to me, and til I do, I'm gonna sit right here and yell about it! Come on, Nancy! My furniture, my family heirlooms, and a new pick-up truck! Until that's settled, here I sit!

NANCY. Well, I wouldn't sit on them boxes, Coleman, if I were you.

COLEMAN. Oh, you wouldn't, would you? *(He sits there. He kicks them.)*

NANCY. And I wouldn't kick them like that, neither.

COLEMAN. Oh, yeah? Well, who's going to stop me? *(He kicks the boxes, hard.)*
NANCY. Keep on kicking. You'll find out. *(Coleman kicks the boxes, and bounces up and down on them, in a tantrum. Suddenly, from inside the boxes comes an unmistakable sound: the electrifying thrushing crackle, the sound of a rattlesnake. Coleman rockets up off the boxes. He looks through a crack in the side of one.)*
COLEMAN. Snakes! Jesus Christ! *(He looks again. The people watch him in a great silence.)* There's rattlesnakes in these boxes! Diamond god damned backed rattlesnakes! And copperheads! Deadly serpents! They're poison! They'll kill you! *(The people all stare at Coleman, and his discovery, saying not a word.)* What are they doing in — *(Pause. Silence. Realization.)* My god. You're Pentecostal Church Snakehandlers. *(Coleman stares at the worshippers of Amalgamation Church. The worshippers stare at Coleman.)*
BUCKHORN. Amen, son.
CONGREGATION. Amen.

(BLACKOUT.)

29

ACT II

As before.

COLEMAN.   Pentecostal Church of God Snakehandlers. Maniacs, Canfield. *(To Reverend Buckhorn.)* You pick up them snakes? Hold them in your hands?

BUCKHORN.   That has been known to happen.

COLEMAN.   And you jump all around, and praise Jesus with rattlesnakes?

NANCY.   Coleman, you're getting it wrong, as usual.

COLEMAN.   Well, what's the trick? There's got to be one. You drug them snakes? Or you milk them first? Or what?

NANCY.   Coleman, they are the way God made them. Full of speed, fangs, and poison death. But that ain't the point.

COLEMAN.   Oh, don't tell me those — *(Pause.)* Wait a minute. I did read something about a man just last —

BONNIE.   Gilbert Letty. He almost died.

CANFIELD.   And before that. Haven't some people — its been in the papers —

BUCKHORN.   *(Soberly.)* That has been known to happen. We don't deny it.

BONNIE.   They think they have faith. When the test comes, they don't.

COLEMAN.   Why, you're breaking the law. There's a state law against using snakes in church! Daddy, you're just breaking the law every way you turn.

BUCKHORN.   State law is not the last word, young Mr. Shedman.

The freedom of our religion is not something state governments care to trifle with. We are left alone, most of the time.

COLEMAN. But it *is* against the law? People have died?

BUCKHORN. *(Nods.)* Yes. *(CARL SPECTER, troubled by COLEMAN, tries to explain.)*

CARL. You're confused. You don't understand. When something is real, then something is real. *(Pause.)* Like her. See, she was smart as a whip. She was swift as the wind. Always sad when I left her, and happy to see me home again. When she'd hunt, and lose sight of me in heavy brush, she'd jump! jump! as she ran, jump' as she ran, like that. She always found me, too! What does the law have to do with it?

COLEMAN. I'm confused?

BUCKHORN. *(Softly.)* Bonnie. *(Bonnie touches Carl gently on the arm. Docile, he turns to her. She leads him away from Coleman.)*

BONNIE. Not now, Carl. Come sit with me.

BUCKHORN. But you are right in this, Mr. Shedman. Many question us. Write articles in newspapers. But the truth is, we only do what God plainly told us to do. It is right here in the Bible, in the words of the Lord. Yet other churches say it isn't. Why they can't read, I don't know. But we can read. We know what we need, and what we want!

COLEMAN. Yes, and so do I. Here it comes, Canfield, right about now.

BUCKHORN. What's that?

COLEMAN. I know what you really want, preacher. And you'll use snakes, elephants, anything that moves, to get it. It is now time, friends, for the holy offering! That's what you want! Gimme, gimme!

NANCY. Oh, Coleman! Don't!

BUCKHORN. Are you saying what I think you are saying?

COLEMAN. I sure am. You ain't getting a thin dime out of me, Daddy!

BUCKHORN. See that bucket?

COLEMAN. What bucket?

BUCKHORN. Way back there against that wall. See it?

31

COLEMAN. What about it?

BUCKHORN. That's our offering plate, in this church. We leave it back there. Nobody even has to look at it, much less put money in it, if they don't want to. We'd rather have no church at all than one built on money.

ALL. Yes, that's right. Yes.

BUCKHORN. *(To everyone.)* Go out into the churches of this world! Whose high and mighty preachers say we are crazy. Why, they have people carrying money-plates stuffed with dollar bills and pledges and silver, and they stick it right up into God's face, and sing a hymn. It is enough to make you vomit on the cross! *(To Coleman, mad.)* Now, you put your thin dime in that bucket, or don't. In your own kind of talk, we don't give a flying fuck what you do with your money! *(Furious, Buckhorn checks himself.)* I swore at this man. Not his fault. I lost my temper, curse of my life. Help me, friends. Don't let me sink in the swamps of anger! *(He lets out a tremendous, hair-raising scream.)* OOOOOOOOOOOOO HHHHHHHHHHHH! GOD! OOOOOOOHHHH GOD!!! *(He falls to his knees, at the altar. Oby jumps to his side.)*

OBY. You all right, Daddy? *(Buckhorn reaches up for his son's hand. Oby grips it hard, and steadies his father.)*

BUCKHORN. Help me, son!

OBY. I'm here, Daddy.

BUCKHORN. Help me, friends! I'm lost! Lost in anger! *(He holds out his arms to them, abandoning his service and role of preacher completely. They rush to him, grab his hands, press them hard.)* Mrs. Wall! Sing something! Help me! *(Mrs. Wall plays "Softly and Tenderly Jesus is Calling." They all move to the piano and sing, while Nancy goes at Coleman.)*

ALL. *(Singing.)*

Softly and tenderly, Jesus is calling,
Calling for you, and for me,
See on the portals He's waiting and watching,
Watching for you and for me.

Come home, come home, you who are weary, come home,

Earnestly, tenderly, Jesus is calling,
Calling, O sinner, come home!
NANCY. See, Coleman! You ain't the only one who gets mad.
You ain't the only one who has troubles.
COLEMAN. Nancy, listen. Come on with me. I'll get you out of
this craziness. I want a divorce, but I don't want to leave you in no
insane asylum.
NANCY. *(In sudden tears.)* It's you who's in the insane asylum!
(She moves away, hiding her feelings.)
ALL. *(Singing.)*
O for the wonderful love He has promised,
Promised for you and for me,
Though we have sinned, He has mercy and pardon,
Pardon for you and for me.
*(As they sing, the congregation pulls at Buckhorn, and calls him
home.)*
COME HOME, COME HOME, you who are weary, come home,
Earnestly, tenderly, Jesus is calling,
Calling, O sinner, come home!
*(Buckhorn, restored, now takes over his service again. We can see now,
under his calm, he is a fractured man, who must struggle against
violent passions.)*
BUCKHORN. Thank you, friends, and praise God. When we ask
him together, He takes away our hate. Don't we know, you can't
get rid of it by yourself. It just grows. *(To Coleman.)* God bless you.
If I anger you calling you son, you anger me calling me Daddy.
COLEMAN. I won't do it again.
BUCKHORN. Then, brother, let's put it this way. We are both
equal creatures of God. You may not like that, and I don't reckon I
do, neither, but that's the way God made us. *(He looks at Coleman
differently now, seeing something new in him.)* It may seem strange to
you, but I've seen you before. Yes, I can see my own eyes, years
ago, looking out of your face. But never mind that now. *(To his congregation.)* What do we know about the mysterious ways of God?
Nothing. We only seek Him, and we won't get scared by what
we find.

ALL. No, we won't. We won't be afraid. Praise the Lord!

BUCKHORN. Now, glory to God! Praise his holy name. So the spirit can move! *Glory* to God! *(Mrs. Wall starts the chord of a hymn, then stops.)*

MRS. WALL. Young man! You, young man!

COLEMAN. You talking to me?

MRS. WALL. Yes, I am. Reverend Buckhorn?

BUCKHORN. Go right ahead, Mrs. Wall. Friends, when you have something to say in this church, you say it.

MRS. WALL. You're just the kind of young person that caused me — well, I'm just — oh! *(She bangs a discordant chord on the piano. Virgil moves to her, and sits on the piano bench with her.)*

VIRGIL. Can I get you a glass of water?

MRS. WALL. No, Virgil. Thank you. *(To Coleman.)* Shady Lane Methodist Church gave me a Timex watch and said goodbye. After thirty-one years, I couldn't teach Sunday School anymore. A young preacher who looks something like you did it. He got a girl from the Teacher's College. She plays the flute, and makes beads, and talks about children re-lating to each other, and that's religion now. I was just let loose. I thought I'd die. The only good thing I've ever done in my life was with the Bible. Teaching miracles to children. Virgil here was in my class, when he was a little boy.

VIRGIL. Yes, ma'am. I sure was.

MRS. WALL. But everybody knows better now. Young man, I got desperate. I couldn't find my religion anywhere. I went to a baseball stadium, to hear about the Lord. But it was religion I wanted, not baseball preaching. All empty smiles, and no power. So then one day, I met Virgil again. He brought me here. To these people you don't think much of. Well, let me tell you they can keep their powerhouse preachers and baseball religion. Let them play at Sunday School, with flutes and beads and the silly talk of college girls. Because I don't need to teach children miracles anymore. I found the miracles here. I always believed them, and I was right. *(She plays a chord again, feeling better.)* So you look down your nose all you want to. You bothered me for a minute, but you don't anymore. I'm free of people like you. Glory be to God. *(While she talks and*

plays, Lorena Cosburg moves timidly toward the piano.)
LORENA. Mrs. Wall. That was a thrilling statement.
MRS. WALL. Thank you.
LORENA. I do so enjoy singing with you, and everyone —
I—
MRS. WALL. Thank you, kindly. *(She plays, firmly, "I Love To Tell The Story," indicating for Lorena to join her. After the first verses, she does. Singing.)*
I love to tell the story
Of unseen things above,
Of Jesus and his glory,
Of Jesus and his love.

I love to tell the story,
Because I know 'tis true,
It satisfies my longings,
As nothing else can do.
(Lorena joins her in a duet.)
MRS. WALL & LORENA.
I love to tell the story,
For those who know it best,
Seem hungering and thirsting
To hear it like the rest.

And when, in scenes of glory,
I sing the new, new song,
Twill be the old, old story,
That I have loved so long.
(Mrs. Wall, Lorena, and now Virgil sing the refrain.)
MRS. WALL, LORENA & VIRGIL.
I love to tell the story,
Twill be my song in glory,
To tell the old, old story,
Of Jesus and his love.
(When they are finished, Lorena stands looking at everyone, very moved.)

LORENA. Oh, I did — I want you to know — I don't know how—

BUCKHORN. *(Gently.)* Speak, Mrs. Cosburg. We'll listen.

LORENA. Oh, I can't.

BUCKHORN. In your own good time, then.

LORENA. But I want to! *(Pause.)* They don't know I'm here tonight. My husband, Frank. Or my children. They'll be hurt. They don't understand, like this young man. They look down on people like you. They make fun of you. I've driven past this church, alone, many times. I never had the courage to come in. I just parked, in the dark, and heard you singing. *(Pause.)* My husband tells me what to do. My children tell me what to do. Delivery boys and clerks at the five and ten tell me what to do. The only time I ever crossed anybody in my life was coming here tonight. I want to know what you believe. Because in my life — in my own life — *(Wretched, she's unable to go on.)*

BUCKHORN. Gather your forces, Sister Cosburg. Your life is all right. We're not afraid of it, if you're not. Speak when you please. *(She nods, grateful, and sits down. Buckhorn smiles at her.)* You see, we observe no strict order of worship here. Worship don't have much order to it, not if it's real. No preacher can schedule the Holy Ghost, shorely not me. He *will* come, Sister Cosburg, all the same. The answer to that, is wait, and be ready. *(He looks at Nancy.)* As I am ready. For the Holy Ghost. For my little bride, and the joy of our union! As *I* have waited!

COLEMAN. Hold it. Waited how long? You got a growed up son. Reverend Daddy. Well, sort of a growed up son.

NANCY. Coleman—

COLEMAN. How did you come by him? Santy Claus? Somebody knit him for you one day?

NANCY. Oh, my awful husband! I'm so sorry.

BUCKHORN. It's all right.

NANCY. No, sir. It's not.

COLEMAN. Sir? Sir, Nancy? You gonna call him sir when you get it the way you like it, and grab him by the—

NANCY. Throw him out! Just *throw* him *out!*

BUCKHORN. Now, hush!! *(Pause.)* Throw him out? Young man out? Well, I'd like to. He attacks my church, and flaunts his carnal knowledge of my young bride in my face. I must confess, I am tempted. But friend, in forty-three years of Christian ministry, no human soul has ever been cast out of a church by me. *(To Coleman, boiling.)* Of course, there is a first time for everything!

CANFIELD. Come here, son, and sit down, for goodness sake. Nice people and good friends, you see how my client here, he has his problems.

HART. He just don't know what they are.

RUDD. Orin, ain't it the truth?

HART. Yep.

MRS. WALL. He likes playing bad boy in Sunday School. That's all.

CANCER MAN. He's a good boy. Strong, and good, inside. I can see that.

CARL. *(To Coleman.)* If you could have seen her just once, you'd know what I mean. Thinking about her, you wouldn't get so mad all the time. She was so beautiful. I see her now, all the time, and I don't get so mad anymore. Don't you understand?

BONNIE. Carl. *(She moves him away from Coleman, gently.)*

OBY. Daddy?

BUCKHORN. Yes, son?

OBY. I need to testify. It's about my new job.

BUCKHORN. Do you have to, right now?

OBY. I'd like to, yes, sir.

BUCKHORN. Well, all right. Make it short.

OBY. Friends, I want to tell you something about the religious nature of bowling. I don't know if you've ever seen the quality of hardwood they have now in a first class bowling alley. It's beautiful. That clear, pure wood, with just the balls rolling down, rolling down. And a clean strike, well, it's heaven. I got a steady job today. *Manager,* now of the sixteen lane Bowl-O-Rama Bowling Parlour, off Highway 43, just out of Gardensburg. It's good Christian recreation, for the Glory of God and the health of your bodies, and you can get there easy from here. I hope you'll all come, and enjoy it,

37

like I do. Praise God. Thank you, Daddy. *(He sits.)*

BUCKHORN. Did you say manager?

OBY. Yes, sir!

BUCKHORN. Well, congratulations. But how can you be in church twice a week, too?

OBY. The owners agreed to that. I don't know how to explain it, but they just go together, Jesus and bowling.

COLEMAN. *(Shaking his head.)* I told you somebody knitted him one day. And that is the man stole my wife for his Daddy. You ain't got a Momma around for me anywhere, have you?

OBY. Now, don't you talk about my Momma!

COLEMAN. Why not? She can't talk for herself, evidently. What happened to her.

OBY. She died.

COLEMAN. Of confusion?

OBY. Of distemper! When I was the littlest boy. After the other one, and before—

BUCKHORN. Son!

OBY. Sir?

BUCKHORN. No need to go into all that.

COLEMAN. Whoa! After the *other* one? Other what?

OBY. Wife, of course. Daddy's first. Before my Momma.

BUCKHORN. Son—

COLEMAN. And when she died, what? How many more?

BUCKHORN. There is no need at this time to go into — uh — these details!

COLEMAN. Oh, no? Just how many wives you had, Reverend Daddy?

BUCKHORN. That is none of your business!

COLEMAN. How many, Nancy? Do you know?

NANCY. *(Shaken.)* I thought I did.

COLEMAN. Well, let's see. One before Oby's Ma, plus Oby's Ma, that's two. One after that, that's three. Three? *(No answer.)* Four? *(No answer. Coleman beams.)* Five? *(Coleman raises his arms.)* Glory to God. *Six?*

BUCKHORN. *(With dignity.)* Taken by the Lord.

OBY. Except the fifth. She ran off, taken by Satan!

BUCKHORN. Hush!

NANCY. *(Weakly.)* Six?

COLEMAN. Didn't he tell you that?

NANCY. Only about — two.

BUCKHORN. I would have, little bride. You know that.

COLEMAN. Sure. In the kitchen, after the wedding, while she's chopping wood, cooking hot bread, and washing babies. *(Pause.)* Babies.

OBY. *(Grinning.)* Been plenty of them.

BUCKHORN. Son!

COLEMAN. How many is plenty? How many children you got, Daddy?

BUCKHORN. My offspring number seventeen children, thirty-one grandchildren, and — a number of great-grandchildren.

COLEMAN. And six mommas in the cemetery, all wore out. Nancy, I know you wanted babies, but are you ready for this?

BUCKHORN. Little bride, you know I will treat you gently.

NANCY. *(Stunned.)* Six? I'm number seven?

BONNIE. Nancy, never you mind that. He is a good man. Life is hard for women, sometimes, yes. But it is better to marry. It is always better to marry.

NANCY. *(Hushed.)* But you never did.

BONNIE. Oh. Yes, I did. But it took me too long, you see, to sort out my — carnal nature. I didn't know what I was doing. *(She looks at the rest, and testifies.)* I had it all mixed up with everything else. You see, there was always my sister, Joann. She was the real beauty. Not me. Now, Joanna never liked going to church. She said it was dull. So *I* did. I went to church all the time. And if any good Christian boy asked for it, up went my skirts for him every time. I did enjoy it. I always liked an enthusiastic Christian boy. And when Joann would say, "Isn't church dull?" I'd say, "Yes, Joann. Of course, Joann." *(She smiles, and remembers her sister.)* Yes, Joann. Of course, Joann. But then, Joann got married, to a boy going to be a doctor, and moved away, and there I was, still in church, still giving it out, and giving it out, until nobody wanted it. The boys became men, and there I was, still in church, dressed like a little girl, ready to do anything anybody wanted. But the men got tired of me. So I found me another church, and another, and sooner or later, every church I joined, I had to leave. Everybody lost their enthusiasm with me, even the plumber husband I finally got, wherever he is now. And Joann married, her children growing up, telling me not to be such a churchmouse. *(Pause.)* Yes, Joann. Of course, Joann. *(Smiles.)* Well, I won't tell a lie. I'll still give it away, to a good enthusiastic boy. But I found something better than that, finally. A real church. Stronger than anything. That's what I wanted to tell Joann. What happens here. *(To Nancy.)* You're still so young. Marry. *(She turns away. Canfield jumps up.)*

CANFIELD. That was deeply moving. I have a daughter I wish had half your sense.

BONNIE. Thank you. What's your daughter's name?

CANFIELD. Hester.

BONNIE. That's a pretty name. Is she a pretty girl?

CANFIELD. She used to be. I used to be a smart looker myself.

BONNIE. I bet you did.

CANFIELD. Then I got my heart condition. Stopped shaving every day, and shining my shoes, after that. One thing led to another. Now I look like this.

BONNIE. You look all right now. You just need sprucing up a little bit. Somebody to wash a shirt for you now and then. Having a heart condition don't mean you can't use it anymore. You can still praise God, and have good times, with new friends.

CANFIELD. I think you're right! Come sit by me. *(She does.)*

COLEMAN. Canfield, don't forget about my divorce!

CANFIELD. Later. We're in church.

COLEMAN. Church, hell. It's a sideshow! *(To Buckhorn.)* When are you going to pull out them snakes?

BUCKHORN. That's not for us to say.

COLEMAN. Well, who, then?

BUCKHORN. The Holy Ghost, Mr. Shedman. *(Bothered, Orin*

40

Hart gets up and goes to Coleman.)

HART. I want to tell this boy. Sonny, what you think you are, you ain't. *I* was that. Ain't that right, Howard?

RUDD. Yep.

HART. And if it hadn't been for this man, and these people, I would have — and I *still* get like that, when I see some young — ah, yet if I couldn't come here, I'd — ah. Howard! *(He turns to Rudd, who grips him firmly by the shoulders. They embrace.)*

RUDD.It's all right, Orin. It ain't going to happen. *(He comforts him. Everybody is respectfully silent, except Coleman.)*

COLEMAN. Fags, by god. Queers.

CANFIELD. Well, son, so what?

COLEMAN. But what are they doing in church? Why ain't they in a bus station somewheres?

CANFIELD. *(To Bonnie.)* What he don't know would fill a book.

BONNIE. Amen.

CANFIELD. Lots of men love another man, somewhere along the line. I did, once. It didn't hurt nobody.

COLEMAN. Canfield? You?

CANFIELD. Praise God, son. Shut up and listen. *(Carl Specter who has been watching Coleman and trying to explain something to him, now erupts.)*

CARL. Yes, praise God! Praise God!! *(He stands shaking, staring at Coleman.)*

BONNIE. *(Softly.)* Oh, Carl.

BUCKHORN. *(Quietly.)* Let him be. *(Carl has his say. Billy perhaps picks out simple chords on his guitar, for awhile.)*

CARL. I tell you again, she come into my life so easy, just like the sun shining down through some cloudy day, making this world bright, that was always dark, for me. From nowhere, out of that City Dump where I found her there in the shoe box with all her dead brothers and sisters around her, and I took her home, and fed her the milk with a hospital glass straw, and she lived. I brought her up. I come to believe there was great blood in her. I trained her. I entered her in the County Puppy Stakes, and she won. Then, in a

41

year, the State Wide Field Trial. Oh, god, could she hunt. They braced her with a lemon-eyed pointer. Right off, he found a covey. But the quail commenced to walk on him. He didn't know what to do. Like a flash, she run the absolute otherway. *What kind of bird dog is that, Carl?* all the rich hunters said, big sportsmen, in their jackets and shiny boots. But I had faith. In just a minute, back she came a-running, having circled them birds in the joy of her smart mind. She boxed them quail in between her and that pointer. The judges said, *She has it, Carl,* and I flushed the quail and shot, and got one, and she retrieved it so dainty, set it in my hand with not one feather missing. Looking up into my eyes, saying, *Well, Carl, I guess we showed them this time,* me saying, *Yes, my honey bee, I think we did.* Off she run to the hunt again, and she won first place, the blue ribbon and the silver cup, and they poisoned her that night. *(Billy stops playing.)* Fed her ground-up glass in hamburger meat. All night long, she couldn't even lie down. I was on my knees with her, every time she heaved and coughed. My baby. And she died. Why did they do that? We never done them hunters no harm. I didn't think there could be anything else for me, but her. *(He nods at Coleman.)* I filled up with hate. Like you. Orin Hart brought me here. Nothing happened the first time, or the second, or the third. But then, I don't remember just when, I saw her again. She come right in that door, looking for me. And when we pray to Jesus, and the serpents are taken up, she's here. And so I live again, in the blood of Jesus, who conquers hateful men, and gave me back my darling in this church. I praise his name forever. Glory to him, for his goodness to me. *(Carl stands nodding at Coleman. There is a pause. Nobody speaks.)* Now I got to go outside, to the bathroom. Excuse me. *(He exits.)*

NANCY. Don't you see, Coleman? Don't you see?

COLEMAN. Yes, I see. And I ask you all, calm and sensible. Is that man crazy, or is he not?

NANCY. Not, Coleman, not!

CANFIELD. Depends, son. Depends.

COLEMAN. He's a lunatic. And you all know it.

CANCER MAN. Son, say you were him. Your dog you loved like

that, died like that. What would you do?

COLEMAN. I wouldn't go to Jesus. I'd find out who poisoned my dog, and my Daddy and I, we'd break his neck.

CANCER MAN. I thought you said your father was dead, son.

COLEMAN. Yes, he is. I mean, *I'd* find out and *I'd* break his neck.

CANCER MAN. Would that help anything?

COLEMAN. Sure. Me.

CANCER MAN. You just can't get it, can you?

CANFIELD. Maybe *I* can. *(To Buckhorn.)* May I?

BUCKHORN. Yes.

CANFIELD. Client, the man didn't do what you'd want to do. Does that mean he's crazy?

COLEMAN. No.

CANFIELD. He came to church instead. Does that mean he's crazy?

COLEMAN. No.

CANFIELD. He believes he found his dog again.

COLEMAN. *That* means he's crazy!

CANFIELD. It also means there is maybe one man less in the world with a broken neck! Who's crazy?

COLEMAN. You are, lawyer, if you think—

CANFIELD. Depends, depends! *(Orin Hart moves in on Coleman, trembling with the rage that is always with him.)*

HART. Broken necks, is it? That what you want?

COLEMAN. Look, don't you mess with me.

BUCKHORN. Go ahead, Mr. Hart. Mess with him. What the hell.

HART. *(Pointing at Rudd.)* See that man? We met fourteen years ago, working the state roads. Mean, both of us. Hungover every morning, standing around the fires, trying to get warm. First time I saw him, I said, "Listen, mister, you going to hog all that fire, or am I going to put you in it?"

RUDD. I said, "Just try it, mister. They'll put us both out."

HART. We didn't fight each other. We got drunk that night.

RUDD. And took on four paratroopers.

HART. Howard was already married. I was too, soon after that.

RUDD. Orin had trouble with May, right off. He wasn't drinking for fun no more. I'd get him home to her.

HART. And I did the same for Howard. One time Edna left him, and took their little girl Jean with her. Howard clamped a razor blade in a pair of pliers, and tried to cut his throat.

RUDD. No, let's skip that, Orin.

HART. Razor in one hand, goodbye letter in the other. But he was drunk and crying. All he did was make a mess of his throat. See the scars?

RUDD. Orin, I said shut up about this!

HART. No, Howard, I'm going to tell him. And you ain't going to stop me. Because without me, you'd have died.

RUDD. *(Sighs.)* Yep.

HART. I was the one who found him, wanting to die, but couldn't. Suicide. I got him to the hospital. I was cool and calm. But in other times, in my domestic torments, sonny boy, it was Howard come to get me, me screaming, wanting to break to pieces any man come near me, and Howard cool and calm, the only man alive could take me home.

RUDD. Bad ass fighting men. Kill the world.

HART. Fighting all the time, since I was a boy. When I had my family around me, and Howard to hold me back, I managed. Then infernal things happened to me.

RUDD. His boy Wayne William got sick and died. His wife couldn't stop drinking no more than he could. He was under the wheel.

HART. There was a man at the plant, named Jackson. He crossed me. I couldn't stop thinking about him. I knowed I was going to kill him.

RUDD. I knew it, too.

HART. I took to hounding the man.

RUDD. I said, "Orin, don't do it."

44

HART. I said, "You try to stop me, I'll kill you, too." You see, bad ass? What we are from the beginning, it grows in us. It was growing in me. What I wanted all my life. A dead man. I commenced carrying the gun.

RUDD. I couldn't help him! I didn't know what to do!

HART. I showed Jackson the gun. He said, "Why are you doing this to me?" I said, "I don't know. I'm just going to kill you."

RUDD. I had to do something. I got him drunk that night, and stole his gun. I said, "All right. If it's dead men you want, you'll have two of them. Me and you. Because I can't live without you, Orin."

HART. I said, "Why, you fool."

RUDD. I said, "Move. I heard about a place where crazy people play with death, and rattlesnakes. If that's what you want, we'll do it there."

HART. He marched me in this room under my own gun, hidden in his pocket. I thought no other man could yell and scream like me. But when the serpents appeared, I'd never seen nothing like it. And the worship. I remembered my wife and children still alive. I thought about all the men I wanted to kill. And I said, "Oh, this torment will end, or I will!" In the music and the singing, I said, "Give it to me! Jesus Christ, you know my evil heart. Give me that snake, you know I want it!" And I took one up. I held my death here, in these hands. And of all the people in the world that night, the Lord anointed Orin Hart.

RUDD. And Howard Rudd. You see, bad ass? *(They stare at Coleman, who stares back, unmoved.)*

COLEMAN. Sure. I see Orin Hart and Howard Rudd. Ain't they pretty?

RUDD. What the hell you mean?

COLEMAN. I'll tell you. Fruits ain't always like girls. They can look like truck drivers, and be queer, my Daddy always said. I don't care about your damn story. You're fags, using a church to fuck each other. It wasn't no Holy Ghost that annointed you, it was—

HART. *(Enraged.)* Son, if you want to get yourself cold cocked, that man or me, either one—

COLEMAN. *(Furious.)* One at a time, or both together! Come on!

NANCY. Coleman, don't! Stop him!

BUCKHORN. Let them alone. *(Hart moves slowly towards Coleman. Coleman faces Hart. He shoves him.)*

COLEMAN. Come on, queer! I'll bust open your god damned — *(Hart seizes him swiftly, spins him around, holds him up in the air, arms crushing his chest. Coleman is a baby in his arms. Hart lays him on the floor, and holds him down.)*

HART. Don't mock the Holy Ghost, bad ass!

RUDD. Bad ass, when we come in here, we felt the power! Not no foolishness with lead pipes and guns, not no beating and drinking and murder and vice, but the power! I tell you, I seen that roof up there split apart! My mouth dried up. My heart stopped. Down from heaven come the Holy Ghost and I mean he *moved* on us! *That* was the power! And we loved each other, freely, and said we didn't want to die. Because for the first time in all our miserable lives, we knowed what a victory was!

HART. Saved! SAVED! Understand, bad ass? *(They get up, leaving Coleman on the floor.)* We had something new to think about.

RUDD. Glory to God. *(They each stamp a boot by Coleman's head. Nancy rushes to Coleman.)*

NANCY. Are you all right? Did they hurt you?

COLEMAN. *(Hurt.)* I'm all right. *(He gets up. Nancy tries to help him.)*

NANCY. Do you need—

COLEMAN. *(Shakes her off.)* I'm all right! *(He stands facing them all. Re-enter Carl.)* So beat me up. I still say this is a sideshow. And I want my legal rights. *(Shaken.)* I won't be put off by lunatics in a circus!

BUCKHORN. Friend, we've all lost our tempers with you tonight. We won't do it again. But after what you've heard, how can you call this a circus?

COLEMAN. *(Almost crying.)* Because you're fakes. My Daddy would know. What you do with them snakes is a lie. Unless you want somebody to get bit, and die. You drug them, or something.

And then you go crazy in here.

BONNIE. *(Terribly upset.)* *Want* somebody to die? Did you say—

BUCKHORN. Just a minute. *(He slowly takes out a faded newspaper clipping from his pocket. He opens it and smooths it reverently, and shows it to Coleman.)* The white haired man on the floor was named George Hensley. In nineteen hundred and nine, on White Oak Mountain, he was the first to read in the Bible, "They shall take up serpents," and then go out and *do* it. He founded the Dolley Pond Church of God, With Signs Following, in Tennessee. He founded this church, in nineteen forty-eight. Yes, people have died. Laws were passed. And we are still here.

BONNIE. Oh, god! Don't I know that!

BUCKHORN. Tell him, Bonnie, if you want to!

BONNIE. Joann's happiness didn't last. My sister got desperate, too, just like the rest of us. I brought her here. I told her not to move without the power. But she did. She cried out and grabbed a snake and he bit her. She stood right here, his fangs in her arm, hanging from her. She said she'd never go to a hospital. Her faith in Jesus Christ would save her life. She would trust in Him. We prayed with her. She commenced to swell. Her color changed. We made her go to the hospital. But that night, Jesus took her. *(She weeps.)* She's with Him now, in heaven. Awful things were said about me. My own family tried to have me arrested. But I'm still here. I still worship in this church! *(She weeps.)* Some people say I killed my own sister! It's not so! I brought her to God! I brought her to God! *(She is touched by Canfield, and held and comforted by him.)*

BUCKHORN. We are persecuted. We are against man's law. George Hensley, who led us to his church finally died, and of snakebite. But he'd been bit and lived over four hundred times! *(Passionately.)* You don't believe it? All right, don't! Lots of people like you say we're crazy, to need this worship this strong this bad! But we do! That is our nature! The Lord Jesus understood us, and in his own sacred word, he told us what to do. *(He points to the altar.)* You see that jar? On the altar, by the cross. That is strychnine poison. If your faith in Jesus Christ is strong enough, you can drink

47

that, and live. That's what the Bible says. You can walk through fire, and not be harmed. That's what the Bible says. You can take up serpents, and not be harmed. That's what the Bible says, and that's what we believe, whether *you* do or not! Stay here, if you want. But don't let me hear you say anything more about a circus! *(Buckhorn mops his brow.)* Mrs. Wall. Give us a hymn, in the name of the Lord. Something quiet. To calm us down. And prepare us for the worship, which I am not holding up no longer. Little bride, I can see you wavering in the faith. Your husband has touched you hard, and filled you with doubt. I never said life with a servant of God is easy. I said it is life. You make up your mind about me and about your husband, and do it now. *(He turns his back on her and Coleman and Oby. The congregation gathers around Buckhorn and Mrs. Wall. They chat quietly, and then sing a gentle hymn.)*

OBY. *(To Nancy.)* You're still worried by your husband, aren't you?

NANCY. *(Miserable.)* Yes.

OBY. Well, talk to him. Maybe you best think again. *(He moves away, to the others. Coleman and Nancy are left alone.)*

COLEMAN. It wasn't just that night, or that man.

NANCY. No.

COLEMAN. When did you decide to leave me? *(He moves close to her. She moves back.)* I won't touch you.

NANCY. I decided lots of times. One night, you hit me.

COLEMAN. I'll never do it again.

NANCY. That's what you said then. And you stuck a little snapshot of me in the frame of that big picture of your momma and daddy and said, see, I love you.

COLEMAN. Well, I did.

NANCY. But I can't live in no picture frame of your momma and daddy! If I'm going to be put in a coffin like that, I want my own children to do it!

COLEMAN. I never said we wouldn't have children.

NANCY. You didn't have to. It was plain enough. *(The congregation sings softly. They sing hymns like "What a Friend We Have In*

48

Jesus" and "In The Garden," hymns old, familiar and quietly passionate, while Coleman and Nancy have it out.)

COLEMAN. I can see why you left me. I can see why you're here. But this crazy religion is a lie, Nancy. It just ain't true.

NANCY. How can you tell?

COLEMAN. Because I won't lie to myself! With everything else wrong about him, my Daddy taught me to see life as it is! And it is mostly god-awful hard! *That's* the truth. Never mind snakes and Jesus. We just have to grow up, and grit our teeth, and face it!

NANCY. Without nothing? No love, no children, nothing?

COLEMAN. We could have that, woman, if you'd just shut up about it!

NANCY. And that your Daddy taught you! Shut up, woman! When are you going to learn something for yourself?

COLEMAN. All right. Here I am. There they are. What is wrong about me, without something just as wrong about them?

NANCY. You drink whiskey and beer.

COLEMAN. Yes. But I don't see dead dogs or roofs splitting open.

NANCY. You curse all the time.

COLEMAN. Yes. But I don't whine, or cry, or beg help from Jesus, like a coward.

NANCY. You hate me.

COLEMAN. No, I don't!

NANCY. And hate yourself!

COLEMAN. All right. Sometimes. And I work and slave at that miserable fish farm my Daddy left me, that I'm scared to leave. I admit that.

NANCY. And it's work, drink, fish, drink, come home, drink, hit me, drink, and try to make love. That's what you call facing life?

COLEMAN. It's honest! *(Shaken.)* Life is hard!

NANCY. Too hard for me, with you. It's not that I didn't come to care for you. I did.

COLEMAN. Do you now?

NANCY. *(A great sigh.)* Oh, I don't know. I thought I'd just walk out of my Momma and Daddy's house and into my husband's house, and have his babies, and it would all be like it was again. And instead of my sisters and brothers and Momma and Daddy, there would be my children and my husband, all around the fire, saying, "We love you, Momma. Welcome home." But what a dream. *(She smiles wanly at him.)* So I picked my husband — you are right about that Sunday School picnic, Coleman — it was a trap I laid for you with my perfume and lace. You walked in it just like a rabbit, and I kicked it shut, But then, my husband was a man with his dreams, too, full of thorns, and so different from mine. So I cried. And this big angel appeared named Oby, and he led me to Reverend Buckhorn, who made me feel safe at home again, with him, and the church, and the serpents. So I trusted again. Most of the time. *(Pause.)* Six wives? *(Pause. Doubtfully.)* I've learned a lot. I think.
COLEMAN. Nancy, I got you into this. I'll get you out. You can't marry that old man. You know what he is now. How many times you seen an old buzzard like that, wearing out his wives? He'll work you to death. I can't let that happen to you. Come home.
NANCY. What?
COLEMAN. We'll talk. I promise I'll never hit you again. Never.
NANCY. What about your divorce?
COLEMAN. We'll talk about it first. Sort it out, like Canfield says. I'll listen to everything you have to say.
NANCY. Coleman, you won't.
COLEMAN. Everything you say. I'll treat you kindly, and gentle. I'll be a good husband. I won't drink. I won't swear. I'll try to quit the fish farm, and get another job. What else? I might even take you to church.
NANCY. What? *(Behind them, the congregation has stopped singing, and has been listening to them.)*
COLEMAN. Some decent church. Near home. Hear that? I will! I'll even pray with you. See what I'll do for you? Praise the Lord. Praise the Lord! Help us poor sinners, O Lord! See, I can do that.

Praise the Lord! Praise the Lord!

CONGREGATION. Amen! Amen, brother! Praise the Lord!! *(Coleman wheels about. He sees they have all been listening to him.)*

COLEMAN. *(Enraged.)* What the hell do you mean, listening in on us? I ain't praying in this place! I'm trying to talk to my god damn stupid wife!! *(And he hits her. Nancy sprawls onto the floor, and Coleman leaps after her.)* Ah, Nancy! *(Nancy holds up her hand, keeping both Coleman and the people away from her.)*

NANCY. See, honey? What would be different? *(She gets up by herself.)* You can have the furniture. I owe you a pick-up truck. Goodbye, Coleman. *(She moves away. Coleman stands shaking. Carl approaches him.)*

CARL. Hit me. Make you feel better.

COLEMAN. *(Choking.)* I don't hit lunatics.

CARL. Just your wife. You think I'm crazy. But I heard you talking about your Daddy. I understand.

COLEMAN. *(Bitterly.)* Oh, yes? Who was yours?

CARL. God is my father. Everybody's here, but yours. He is Jesus's father, too, and His right arm is the Holy Ghost. You're still praying to your mortal father, who's dead. That's bad. *(He holds open his arms.)* I'm crazy. Hit me. *(The people call Carl back. Canfield approaches Coleman.)*

CANFIELD. Your lawyer can't help you. He's converted. To find friends like this at my time of life and in the condition of my heart, is not something I'm going to hesitate about. *(He turns to Bonnie.)* I'm leaving you, client. You can prove desertion now, by your wife *and* your lawyer. I wish — well, good luck. *(Cancer Man approaches Coleman.)*

CANCER MAN. They cut me to pieces. I'll be dead, soon, like your daddy. That's all right. You don't have to worry about that. *(Coleman breaks. He sobs, grabs a box or a chair, and sobbing, at the same time filled with black rages, smashes it. He cries out and sobs: "Mama! Daddy!" It is useless. He kneels amid his little ruin, trembling and weeping.)*

BUCKHORN. Yes. We wish we could tell you what to do. We can't. We're in this trouble, too, and have to do for ourselves the best we can. *(He turns to the congregation.)* Preachers talk. What can a preacher tell a soul suffering like that? What can they tell any of us? Nothing. We know it is hopeless. *(He begins his service.)* All we can do is worship. All we can do is turn to the Lord, Who understood us. Because when He rose up into heaven, He spoke, to them who believed in Him, to them He left behind. We turn to those words! What are they, friends? Read me the words of Jesus Christ! *(Virgil Tides goes to the lectern. He reads from a Bible.)*

VIRGIL. The Book of Mark. Chapter 16, verses 17 and 18. "And these signs shall follow them that believe. In my name shall they cast out devils."

ALL. *(Softly.)* Amen.

VIRGIL. "They shall speak with new tongues — "

ALL. *(Stronger.)* Amen!

VIRGIL. "They shall take up serpents — "

ALL. Amen! Glory to God!

VIRGIL. "And if they drink any deadly thing, it shall not hurt them — "

ALL. No! Never! Amen!

VIRGIL. "They shall lay hands upon the sick — "

ALL. Amen! Praise God!

VIRGIL. "And they shall recover!"

ALL. Praise God! Amen! Glory to God! Praise the Lord! *(From reading the Bible, Virgil in a furious rapture begins to speak in tongues. The strange syllables are pure emotion, erupting from him with great force, twisting his body.)*

VIRGIL. Ah! Ah! Sha — *gon* — du — lah! Sha — *gon* — du — lah!! Ma — shill — a *hon* — du — lah!! Gos — la! Gos — la! *(Possessed, Virgil speaks in tongues. He goes to the boxes of rattlesnakes, and opens one of them. We hear the snakes rattling. Virgil takes one out and holds it up. [The snakes should be mimed, not real.] He stares at it, crying out in tongues.)* Ah — gall — a sonda! Ah — gall — a sonda! Eee — ma — nona! Eee — ma — nona! La — gall — la — sa! La — gall — la sa!!! *(He puts the snake back in the box. He collapses exhausted at Buckhorn's feet.)*

BUCKHORN. I remember! I thought I would die. But the

heavens came open, and wave after wave of God's love broke over me! I held the serpent, and I spoke in tongues! *(They embrace.)* God bless you, Virgil! God bless you, son! *(Cancer Man is at the boxes. He takes out a serpent. He holds it up high, and approaches Coleman.)*

CANCER MAN. You see! I'm still alive! They said my life was over! But I feel the power of the Lord. I hold the serpent! I defeat him! God gives me this victory! I feel wonderful! *(He holds the snake out to Coleman.)* And see. The snake is calm. *(He turns, puts it back in the box. Nancy moves away from everyone. The people begin to sing, "Stand Up, Stand Up For Jesus.")*

ALL. *(Singing.)*
Stand up, Stand up for Jesus
Ye soldiers of the cross,
Lift high His royal banner,
It must not suffer loss!

From victory unto victory,
In this His glorious day,
You that are men now serve—

(Billy Boggs rips out a discordant chord on his guitar, and cries out. The singing stops. Billy goes to Coleman. He stares at him hard.)

BILLY. I didn't start out this way! You ain't the only one! I don't want my wife! I don't want my baby! That's the truth! You hear that, Muriel?

MURIEL. Yes. I do.

BILLY. All I meant to do was work in town during the day and play my guitar here at night. That's why I come. Then I met Muriel here. We got in trouble. I did what I thought was right. We got married. But it's not right now! *(He shakes with rage.)* I'm trapped! I can't stand it! Sometimes I hate her! Sometimes I hate — ah, how can I do that! I wouldn't hurt my own child!!! *(The people move aside for him. He approaches the boxes.)* Oh, god, they scare me.

BUCKHORN. Billy, you don't reach in every time. You wait for the Lord.

BILLY. I can be free. Lord Jesus, anoint me. Give me the power.

(He takes a deep breath.) I believe. I'm not afraid. *(A hideous rattle. He takes out a huge rattlesnake. He holds it directly in front of his face.)* Strike. Kill me, if you can. *(He holds the snake, shuddering with terror.)*

ALL. Praise God! Glory to God, Billy!

BILLY. There! There! Oh, Holy Ghost! *(He puts the snake back in the box, and turns to his wife.)*

MURIEL. God bless you, Billy. *(They move aside together, with the baby. Coleman gets up.)*

COLEMAN. Get out of my way! Get out of my way!

NANCY. No, Coleman! No!

BUCKHORN. There's death in that box!

HART. You'll risk your life!

RUDD. You'll put it on the line!

CANCER MAN. If you believe, you'll live!

BUCKHORN. But if you don't, you can die! Right here. *(At the boxes, Coleman spreads wide his arms.)*

COLEMAN. Then I'll die! Right here! *(He reaches down into the boxes. He pulls out two rattlesnakes, and holds them up. They rattle, loudly. He steps forward, staring at them, in stark terror. He turns about, holding them. Convulsions rack him. But when he turns to us again, his face is amazed. He looks up, past the snakes. Coleman cries out. He is converted.)*

BUCKHORN. Praise the Lord! He made us! We are His! *(The people now begin to erupt within themselves. Some are seized by spasms, some shaken by convulsions, some sing, some dance.)* People say we're crazy! People say Jesus never meant us to *do* what he said! And we say, what do you know about Jesus and his ways! Nothing! Nothing! *(Mrs. Wall has a snake in her hands. She and Bonnie face the terrified, but thrilled, Lorena.)*

MRS. WALL. Sister!

LORENA. Yes, sister?

MRS. WALL. *(To Bonnie.)* Tell her! Tell her!

BONNIE. The first time I seen the snakes, I nearly died. I couldn't run. I couldn't move. I stood there, praying. Then the Holy Ghost gave me the power!

LORENA. What's it like? I want to know!

BONNIE. Your hands get numb.

LORENA. Yes?

BONNIE. Then they get cold.

LORENA. *Yes?*

BONNIE. Then they begin to itch!

LORENA. Oh, *yes!* I never felt like this before!

MRS. WALL. Do your hands itch now, sister?

LORENA. They do!

BONNIE. Then, if you have the power, grab him.

MRS. WALL. It's the best feeling you'll ever have!

LORENA. Give it to me! Give it — *(They hand her a huge rattle-snake. All three hold it. They scream with pleasure.)*

LORENA, BONNIE & MRS. WALL. Ah! Ah! AHHH!!! O, God in heaven! O, God in heaven!!! *(Everyone now, except Nancy, handles serpents. She sits to one side, silent amid the singing and the shouting. The service reaches its climax. People move about, stamping and shaking the church. Some cry. Some laugh. Some scream and beat the floor. Some dance. Some sing. Some hold up the jar of poison. Some play with fire. They all release to their Lord the tensions and the sorrows of their lives, moving about as if in some tremendous storm. Then they stop. A light shines down on the threadbare altar cloth. A different music is heard: an organ, or perhaps some strange cosmic sound. They all simply look up, stilled, and for a moment, their great God himself comes into their church, and into them. For an instant, they are blessed, and delivered. Then the music becomes again what it was and they revert slowly back to their dancing and singing. Slowly, it subsides. Slowly, the snakes are put back in the boxes. The sobbing, the convulsions, the laughter, the singing and the music stop. They are all exhausted. Silence. Long pause. In a corner, by himself, Cancer Man sags, and kneels. Coleman kneels by Cancer Man. He grips his hand, hard.)*

COLEMAN. It's eating on you, ain't it? And them drugs? *(Cancer Man nods.)* I can tell. Hang on to me. *(Cancer Man nods.)* You ever fish? *(Cancer Man nods again, surprised.)* Want to again. With me? I know where to find them. *(Cancer Man nods.)* Then we'll go. Together. *(Coleman stands. He, Nancy and Buckhorn look at each other.)*

BUCKHORN. Well, young man?

COLEMAN. I want to join the church. Please take me. Don't send me away. *(He sinks to his knees before Buckhorn.)*

BUCKHORN. Well, little bride?

NANCY. I'm leaving. I don't want to be a child no more. And my babies will just have to wait awhile. *(She kisses Buckhorn on the cheek.)* I do thank you. *(She looks at the congregation.)* All of you. I'll come to church again, some day. *(She looks at Coleman, on his knees. She touches him, gently.)* Good luck, Coleman. *(Exit Nancy. Buckhorn stares after her, then at Coleman. He shakes his head.)*

BUCKHORN. She goes. You stay. *(Sighs.)* Blessed be the name of the Lord. *(Coleman weeps quietly. All the people watch. Muriel, sitting with her baby, begins to sing, alone.)*

MURIEL. *(Singing.)*

There is a wideness to God's mercy
Like the wideness of the sea,
There is a strangeness to God's blessing.
Like the thrill of e-ter-ni-ty.

Jesus defend us, O sweet mercy send us,
O angels attend us with unchanging love,
Jesus defend us and sweet mercy send us,
And angels attends us from heaven above.

CURTAIN

PROPERTY PLOT

Bible for Nancy
Pint bottle cheap whiskey for Canfield
Teacups, teapot, small kerosene stove
Wooden boxes, very sturdy
Guitar for Billy
Baby wrapped in blankets for Muriel
Bucket for collection plate
Metal pipe for Oby
Small wooden cross for altar
Mason jar of whitish liquid for altar
Faded newspaper clipping for Buckhorn Sr.
Rubber snakes
Hymnals, piano, fans, for the church
Various musical instruments for those who play them

COSTUMES

The plain clothes of Southern rural people.

MUSIC

The hymns used in the play may be found in any standard hymnal, with the exception of the last, which was put together by the playwright to end the play. It should be sung to the music for the Welsh hymn melody, *Alleluia! Sing to Jesus.*

THE SET

The ground plan may fit any theatre or playing space. It should include a table, later converted into an altar, a smaller table with Nancy's teacups and stove on it, a piano covered with a blanket, sheet or piece of canvas, simple chairs and benches. Lights strung overhead may be turned on when the service begins. The walls of the building may be rough unpainted wood. In any case, the setting should be a simple one, without elaboration, so that it does not detract from the people.

SNAKES

The author suggests, in the strongest possible terms, that the snakes be mimed by the actors, with sounds of rattles. Productions that use real snakes, or even rubber snakes, have not been as successful as those which use and trust the theatrical imagination.

BY ROMULUS LINNEY

PLAYS

The Sorrows of Frederick
The Love Suicide at Schofield Barracks
Democracy
Holy Ghosts
Old Man Joseph and His Family
El Hermano
The Captivity of Pixie Shedman
Childe Byron
The Death of King Philip
Laughing Stock:
      Goodbye, Howard
      F.M.
      Tennessee
The Love Suicide at Schofield Barracks
      (One Act)
Sand Mountain:
      Sand Mountain Matchmaking
      Why the Lord Come to Sand Mountain
A Woman Without A Name
Pops:
      Can Can
      Claire de Lune
      Ave Maria
      Gold and Silver Waltz
      Battle Hymn of the Republic
      Songs of Love
Heathen Valley
Juliet, Yancey and April Snow

NOVELS

Heathen Valley
Slowly, By Thy Hand Unfurled
Jesus Tales

NEW PLAYS

★ **THE EXONERATED by Jessica Blank and Erik Jensen.** Six interwoven stories paint a picture of an American criminal justice system gone horribly wrong and six brave souls who persevered to survive it. "The #1 play of the year...intense and deeply affecting..." *–NY Times.* "Riveting. Simple, honest storytelling that demands reflection." *–A.P.* "Artful and moving...pays tribute to the resilience of human hearts and minds." *–Variety.* "Stark...riveting...cunningly orchestrated." *–The New Yorker.* "Hard-hitting, powerful, and socially relevant." *–Hollywood Reporter.* [7M, 3W] ISBN: 0-8222-1946-8

★ **STRING FEVER by Jacquelyn Reingold.** Lily juggles the big issues: turning forty, artificial insemination and the elusive scientific Theory of Everything in this Off-Broadway comedy hit. "Applies the elusive rules of string theory to the conundrums of one woman's love life. Think *Sex and the City* meets *Copenhagen.*" *–NY Times.* "A funny offbeat and touching look at relationships...an appealing romantic comedy populated by oddball characters." *–NY Daily News.* "Where kooky, zany, and madcap meet...whimsically winsome." *–NY Magazine.* "STRING FEVER will have audience members happily stringing along." *–TheaterMania.com.* "Reingold's language is surprising, inventive, and unique." *–nytheatre.com.* "...[a] whimsical comic voice." *–Time Out.* [3M, 3W (doubling)] ISBN: 0-8222-1952-2

★ **DEBBIE DOES DALLAS adapted by Erica Schmidt, composed by Andrew Sherman, conceived by Susan L. Schwartz.** A modern morality tale told as a comic musical of tragic proportions as the classic film is brought to the stage. "A scream! A saucy, tongue-in-cheek romp." *–The New Yorker.* "Hilarious! DEBBIE manages to have it all: beauty, brains and a great sense of humor!" *–Time Out.* "Shamelessly silly, shrewdly self-aware and proud of being naughty. Great fun!" *–NY Times.* "Racy and raucous, a lighthearted, fast-paced thoroughly engaging and hilarious send-up." *–NY Daily News.* [3M, 5W] ISBN: 0-8222-1955-7

★ **THE MYSTERY PLAYS by Roberto Aguirre-Sacasa.** Two interrelated one acts, loosely based on the tradition of the medieval mystery plays. "... stylish, spine-tingling...Mr. Aguirre-Sacasa uses standard tricks of horror stories, borrowing liberally from masters like Kafka, Lovecraft, Hitchcock...But his mastery of the genre is his own...irresistible." *–NY Times.* "Undaunted by the special-effects limitations of theatre, playwright and *Marvel* comic-book writer Roberto Aguirre-Sacasa maps out some creepy twilight zones in THE MYSTERY PLAYS, an engaging, related pair of one acts...The theatre may rarely deliver shocks equivalent to, say, *Dawn of the Dead*, but Aguirre-Sacasa's work is fine compensation." *–Time Out.* [4M, 2W] ISBN: 0-8222-2038-5

★ **THE JOURNALS OF MIHAIL SEBASTIAN by David Auburn.** This epic one-man play spans eight tumultuous years and opens a uniquely personal window on the Romanian Holocaust and the Second World War. "Powerful." *–NY Times.* "[THE JOURNALS OF MIHAIL SEBASTIAN] allows us to glimpse the idiosyncratic effects of that awful history on one intelligent, pragmatic, recognizably real man..." *–NY Newsday.* [3M, 5W] ISBN: 0-8222-2006-7

★ **LIVING OUT by Lisa Loomer.** The story of the complicated relationship between a Salvadoran nanny and the Anglo lawyer she works for. "A stellar new play. Searingly funny." *–The New Yorker.* "Both generous and merciless, equally enjoyable and disturbing." *–NY Newsday.* "A bitingly funny new comedy. The plight of working mothers is explored from two pointedly contrasting perspectives in this sympathetic, sensitive new play." *–Variety.* [2M, 6W] ISBN: 0-8222-1994-8

DRAMATISTS PLAY SERVICE, INC.
440 Park Avenue South, New York, NY 10016 212-683-8960 Fax 212-213-1539
postmaster@dramatists.com   www.dramatists.com

NEW PLAYS

★ **MATCH by Stephen Belber.** Mike and Lisa Davis interview a dancer and choreographer about his life, but it is soon evident that their agenda will either ruin or inspire them—and definitely change their lives forever. "Prolific laughs and ear-to-ear smiles." *–NY Magazine.* "Uproariously funny, deeply moving, enthralling theater. Stephen Belber's MATCH has great beauty and tenderness, and abounds in wit." *–NY Daily News.* "Three and a half out of four stars." *–USA Today.* "A theatrical steeplechase that leads straight from outrageous bitchery to unadorned, heartfelt emotion." *–Wall Street Journal.* [2M, 1W] ISBN: 0-8222-2020-2

★ **HANK WILLIAMS: LOST HIGHWAY by Randal Myler and Mark Harelik.** The story of the beloved and volatile country-music legend Hank Williams, featuring twenty-five of his most unforgettable songs. "[LOST HIGHWAY has] the exhilarating feeling of Williams on stage in a particular place on a particular night…serves up classic country with the edges raw and the energy hot…By the end of the play, you've traveled on a profound emotional journey: LOST HIGHWAY transports its audience and communicates the inspiring message of the beauty and richness of Williams' songs…forceful, clear-eyed, moving, impressive." *–Rolling Stone.* "…honors a very particular musical talent with care and energy… smart, sweet, poignant." *–NY Times.* [7M, 3W] ISBN: 0-8222-1985-9

★ **THE STORY by Tracey Scott Wilson.** An ambitious black newspaper reporter goes against her editor to investigate a murder and finds the *best* story…but at what cost? "A singular new voice…deeply emotional, deeply intellectual, and deeply musical…" *–The New Yorker.* "…a conscientious and absorbing new drama…" *–NY Times.* "…a riveting, tough-minded drama about race, reporting and the truth…" *–A.P.* "… a stylish, attention-holding script that ends on a chilling note that will leave viewers with much to talk about." *–Curtain Up.* [2M, 7W (doubling, flexible casting)] ISBN: 0-8222-1998-0

★ **OUR LADY OF 121st STREET by Stephen Adly Guirgis.** The body of Sister Rose, beloved Harlem nun, has been stolen, reuniting a group of life-challenged childhood friends who square off as they wait for her return. "A scorching and dark new comedy… Mr. Guirgis has one of the finest imaginations for dialogue to come along in years." *–NY Times.* "Stephen Guirgis may be the best playwright in America under forty." *–NY Magazine.* [8M, 4W] ISBN: 0-8222-1965-4

★ **HOLLYWOOD ARMS by Carrie Hamilton and Carol Burnett.** The coming-of-age story of a dreamer who manages to escape her bleak life and follow her romantic ambitions to stardom. Based on Carol Burnett's bestselling autobiography, *One More Time.* "…pure theatre and pure entertainment…" *–Talkin' Broadway.* "…a warm, fuzzy evening of theatre." *–BrodwayBeat.com.* "…chuckles and smiles of recognition or surprise flow naturally…a remarkable slice of life." *–TheatreScene.net.* [5M, 5W, 1 girl] ISBN: 0-8222-1959-X

★ **INVENTING VAN GOGH by Steven Dietz.** A haunting and hallucinatory drama about the making of art, the obsession to create and the fine line that separates truth from myth. "Like a van Gogh painting, Dietz's story is a gorgeous example of excess—one that remakes reality with broad, well-chosen brush strokes. At evening's end, we're left with the author's resounding opinions on art and artifice, and provoked by his constant query into which is greater: van Gogh's art or his violent myth." *–Phoenix New Times.* "Dietz's writing is never simple. It is always brilliant. Shaded, compressed, direct, lucid—he frames his subject with a remarkable understanding of painting as a physical experience." *–Tucson Citizen.* [4M, 1W] ISBN: 0-8222-1954-9

DRAMATISTS PLAY SERVICE, INC.
440 Park Avenue South, New York, NY 10016 212-683-8960 Fax 212-213-1539
postmaster@dramatists.com   www.dramatists.com

NEW PLAYS

★ **INTIMATE APPAREL by Lynn Nottage.** The moving and lyrical story of a turn-of-the-century black seamstress whose gifted hands and sewing machine are the tools she uses to fashion her dreams from the whole cloth of her life's experiences. "…Nottage's play has a delicacy and eloquence that seem absolutely right for the time she is depicting…" *–NY Daily News*. "…thoughtful, affecting…The play offers poignant commentary on an era when the cut and color of one's dress—and of course, skin—determined whom one could and could not marry, sleep with, even talk to in public." *–Variety*. [2M, 4W] ISBN: 0-8222-2009-1

★ **BROOKLYN BOY by Donald Margulies.** A witty and insightful look at what happens to a writer when his novel hits the bestseller list. "The characters are beautifully drawn, the dialogue sparkles…" *–nytheatre.com*. "Few playwrights have the mastery to smartly investigate so much through a laugh-out-loud comedy that combines the vintage subject matter of successful writer-returning-to-ethnic-roots with the familiar mid-life crisis." *–Show Business Weekly*. [4M, 3W] ISBN: 0-8222-2074-1

★ **CROWNS by Regina Taylor.** Hats become a springboard for an exploration of black history and identity in this celebratory musical play. "Taylor pulls off a Hat Trick: She scores thrice, turning CROWNS into an artful amalgamation of oral history, fashion show, and musical theater…" *–TheatreMania.com*. "…wholly theatrical…Ms. Taylor has created a show that seems to arise out of spontaneous combustion, as if a bevy of department-store customers simultaneously decided to stage a revival meeting in the changing room." *–NY Times*. [1M, 6W (2 musicians)] ISBN: 0-8222-1963-3

★ **EXITS AND ENTRANCES by Athol Fugard.** The story of a relationship between a young playwright on the threshold of his career and an aging actor who has reached the end of his. "[Fugard] can say more with a single line than most playwrights convey in an entire script…Paraphrasing the title, it's safe to say this drama, making its memorable entrance into our consciousness, is unlikely to exit as long as a theater exists for exceptional work." *–Variety*. "A thought-provoking, elegant and engrossing new play…" *–Hollywood Reporter*. [2M] ISBN: 0-8222-2041-5

★ **BUG by Tracy Letts.** A thriller featuring a pair of star-crossed lovers in an Oklahoma City motel facing a bug invasion, paranoia, conspiracy theories and twisted psychological motives. "…obscenely exciting…top-flight craftsmanship. Buckle up and brace yourself…" *–NY Times*. "…[a] thoroughly outrageous and thoroughly entertaining play…the possibility of enemies, real and imagined, to squash has never been more theatrical." *–A.P.* [3M, 2W] ISBN: 0-8222-2016-4

★ **THOM PAIN (BASED ON NOTHING) by Will Eno.** An ordinary man muses on childhood, yearning, disappointment and loss, as he draws the audience into his last-ditch plea for empathy and enlightenment. "It's one of those treasured nights in the theater—treasured nights anywhere, for that matter—that can leave you both breathless with exhilaration and…in a puddle of tears." *–NY Times*. "Eno's words…are familiar, but proffered in a way that is constantly contradictory to our expectations. Beckett is certainly among his literary ancestors." *–nytheatre.com*. [1M] ISBN: 0-8222-2076-8

★ **THE LONG CHRISTMAS RIDE HOME by Paula Vogel.** Past, present and future collide on a snowy Christmas Eve for a troubled family of five. "…[a] lovely and hauntingly original family drama…a work that breathes so much life into the theater." *–Time Out*. "…[a] delicate visual feast…" *–NY Times*. "…brutal and lovely…the overall effect is magical." *–NY Newsday*. [3M, 3W] ISBN: 0-8222-2003-2

DRAMATISTS PLAY SERVICE, INC.
440 Park Avenue South, New York, NY 10016 212-683-8960 Fax 212-213-1539
postmaster@dramatists.com www.dramatists.com